The Au⋯ to Spy

How Government,

Business, and Hackers

Rob Us of Privacy

first edition

Catherine Nolan

Ashley M. Wilson, JD

Published by:
Technics Publications, LLC
2 Lindsley Road
Basking Ridge, NJ 07920 USA
http://www.TechnicsPub.com

Cover design by Mark Brye
Edited by Carol Lehn and Erin Elizabeth Long

ISBN, print ed.9781935504795

First Printing 2014
Library of Congress Control Number: 2014944449

Table of Contents

Introduction
Do I Have Any Personal Data Privacy?

If you feel frustrated about your personal data being misused, hacked or compromised, you are in the majority of Americans. Hacking and the public's concern about their privacy are becoming so commonplace that hacking events no longer warrant a headline in a newspaper but are buried in the Business section or on a blog that most people don't see. Consider these stories, each concerning a different segment of the population, and how their data is being exploited:

> EBay revealed that a cyber-attack carried out months ago has compromised customer data, and the company urged 145 million users of its online commerce platform to change their passwords after hackers stole email addresses, encrypted passwords, birth dates, mailing addresses and other information. [1]

> Schools routinely transfer large quantities of student personal data, including transcript information, homework essays, lunchroom purchases and even student weight, to third party providers. School boards are considering limiting access to yearbooks and student directories after revelations that data aggregators are using student data for marketing purposes. [2]

---

[1] "Hackers nab eBay user data", *Chicago Tribune,* Business Section 2, May 22, 2014, p.3

[2] Center for Information Technology Policy, *Princeton University,* Feb. 6, 2014, https://citp.princeton.edu/event/privacy/

> Farmers are serving notice in Washington that the federal government might need to become involved in yet another debate over electronic security and privacy issues because of the amount data sensors are collecting; sensors are being increasingly used to measure soil conditions, seeding rates, crop yields and many other variables that could be hacked or exploited by corporations or government agencies. Farmers worry that a hedge fund or large company with access to "real-time" yield big data from hundreds of combines at harvest time might be able to use that information to speculate in commodities markets long before the government issues crop-production estimates.[3]

Consider this, too: the vast majority of identities are not stolen intact but with sophisticated tools that can take a fact from one site, an online survey you took on another site and a purchase from third site, and little by little they can piece together your buying habits, your church and school affiliations, the names of your pets, the names of your family, your illnesses, your driving habits, the places you have vacationed and much, much more. This is not science fiction and this is not the future; this is what is happening to each and every one of us now—today. And although the vast majority of adults say they are concerned about providing personal information online, nearly a third say they have never used a privacy setting on their computer, never inquired about the charities to whom they donate their money, never worried about searching for medical information and never thought twice about giving their bank their social security number over the Internet.

---

[3] "American Farmers Confront Big Data Revolution", *FOX News,* Mar. 19, 2014, http://www.foxnews.com/us/2014/03/29/american-farmers-confront-big-data-revolution/

How many of these online activities you have personally preformed?

1. Posted your resume on LinkedIn?

2. Opened an email from someone you didn't know?

3. Kept in touch with your friends on Twitter?

4. Told a site to "Remember Me" so you didn't have to use your password?

5. Checked the Dow or other stock market reports?

6. Posted your vacation destination on Facebook?

7. Download an app on your Smartphone?

8. Used a family member's name as a password?

9. Checked out an article in an online newspaper?

10. Clicked on an ad that popped up while browsing another site?

Numbers 3, 5 and 9 are activities that are relatively harmless, but the rest are susceptible to online tracking and even fraud. Every time you go online, you need to ask yourself, "If someone is monitoring my activity, am I disclosing something I don't want that person to know?"

Okay, you say you are extremely careful to the point where you change your password every two weeks, never pay bills online, don't post on Facebook and won't ever use an ATM. Think that will keep you safe? Don't bet on it. Much of the information about you is in public records; here is some of the "sensitive" information accessible by anyone:

The Data Available in Public Records

As you see, a skilled data broker can amass a lot of information without even breaking into your computer, and a hacker can learn a lot more by accessing your personal online files. Companies are spending millions of dollars yearly to combat hackers and fight off cyber-attacks. JP Morgan Chase spends about $200 million a year to protect its data and expects that figure to climb 20 to 40 percent a year for the next several years.[4] Don't you think it's about time you thought about protecting your own personal data?

---

[4] Quick, Becky, "JP Morgan's $200 Million Problem (and Targets and Yahoo's)", *Fortune*, pg. 88

This book reveals the ways in which your identity and personal data have been stolen by various sources. Rather than worrying about the NSA having your phone calls and emails, worry more about the insidious data brokers that are collecting information about you every time you log on to your laptop, use your cell phone, access an app or use your GPS.

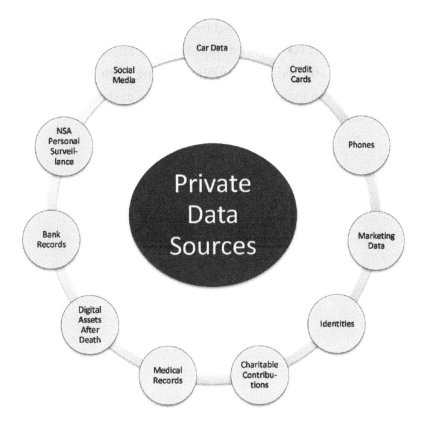

What Data Can Be Compromised?

But more than warning you, we give ways in which you can limit the amount of personal data that is being snatched and then divulged to whomever has a few dollars to buy it. Can you completely cut off the flow of information about yourself? The answer is no, not completely. There is too much data out there already and increasingly sophisticated ways to obtain bits and pieces. But knowing how it is collected gives you the power to limit the information on the sites over which you have control.

One last caveat: laws and regulations are changing rapidly as people become more aware of the assault on personal privacy. While we have used the latest information as of the writing of this book, we caution that you should check your local, state and federal regulations along with your service agreements to make sure you are kept up to date on changes to existing rules and policies.

Chapter 1

Social Media and "The Right to Be Forgotten"

Do you really want all of your personal information to be available to whomever wants to search on Google, Facebook, LinkedIn or one of the other social media sites?

What about those compromising pictures a friend took when you were in college, or the fact that you were once arrested for drunk driving? Did you have to file for bankruptcy when the economy tanked, or have you ever been divorced? How much did your house sell for, and how much do you pay in real estate taxes? Did you vote Republican? What are the names of your pets, your relatives? Did you disclose in one of those dating preference surveys that you like "long walks in the woods," "men who take charge," and "would skinny dip at midnight under a full moon"?

All this, and more, is available online, and you have no way of removing it, whether it is damaging to your career, your marriage or your personal reputation. Eric Posner, University of Chicago law professor, quoted in the *Chicago Tribune*, says, "Privacy allows us to experiment, make mistakes, and start afresh if we mess up. It is this potential for rehabilitation, for second chances, that is under assault from Google."[5]

The chart below illustrates what can be gleaned from some of the most popular internet sites--and most of the sites don't even have to be hacked, we willingly provide the information which can be viewed by countless others.

How Social Media Exposes Your Personal Information

The European Union Court of Justice recently upheld a complaint against Google to have personal information removed from their site. 90 percent of Europe's search market is dominated by Google, and whether or not this ruling is enforceable, the public wants to have some say over what the Internet keeps alive forever. As Time magazine reports, "Make no mistake, this is a watershed moment in human history: mankind, after spending untold millennia looking for ways to be remembered by posterity, must now beg to be forgotten instead."[6]

---

[5] Page, Clarence, "Right to be forgotten' won't fly in USA", Chicago Tribune, May 21, 2014, Section 1, p. 21

[6] Grossman, Lev, "You Have the Right to Be Forgotten", Time, May 26, 2014, p. 17

The European Union aside, experts believe this will never happen in the U.S. because of the First Amendment, which most Americans believe overrides the right to privacy. The Index on Censorship, an international organization promoting free speech, has said, "Before personal data became a commodity mined by corporations and attackers alike, the need for a legal stance on the identity of the 'owner' of data relating to oneself may have seemed laughable. However that has landed us in the situation of today when entities that mine and monetize our data can refer to this very welcome EU ruling as 'disappointing'. Commercially disappointing it may be, however it is a step, albeit a small one, in the right direction."[7]

In an article about social media, Naomi Troni asks, "Was it really just a generation ago that people kept all but their most basic information under virtual lock and key? Today, we happily share our date and place of birth, name of our first pet, mother's maiden name, favorite movie or book, favorite color, first school teacher—and countless other bits of information required by online services as part of their security procedures."[8] Not only do we gladly share all kinds of personal experiences and opinions, but we do it for free. We are so accustomed to providing our opinions about purchases, blogging about our vacations, and taking surveys about our political preferences that we seldom even think

---

[7] Ferguson, Rick, "'Right to be forgotten' is the step in the right direction", Index on Censorship, May 21, 2014, http://www.indexoncensorship.org/2014/05/counterpoint-right-forgotten-step-right-direction/

[8] Troni, Naomi "Social Media Privacy: A Contradiction In Terms?" *Forbes*, Apr. 24, 2012

twice before posting all kinds of what used to be private information. Familiarity has bred complacency and even foolhardiness; we've all heard about people uploading pretty much everything, including the most intimate pictures—images that they wish they could take back. Unfortunately, once it's out there—it's out there!

A European global survey conducted among 7,213 adults in 19 countries found that 55 percent of respondents are worried that "technology is robbing us of our privacy"; the figure was above 60 percent in a number of countries including the United States and China. And it's not just snooping companies and hackers that consumers fear. Nearly half the sample (47 percent)—and a majority of Millennials—worry that friends or family will share inappropriate personal information about them online. Around one third overall already regret posting personal information about themselves.[9]

IS FACEBOOK YOUR "FRIEND" OR "FRENEMY"?

George Bronk looked for email accounts on Facebook pages, then gleaned enough personal information from postings to answer basic "lost" password security questions such as the name of an elementary school or favorite color. After he changed passwords and took over accounts, he would search folders for compromising photos. He would then blackmail women, threatening to email the photos to the families, friends and co-workers of the victims.[10]

---

[9] Troni, Naomi, Ibid

[10] Thompson, Don, "George Bronk Used Facebook to Hack Women's Emails", *Huffington Post*; Jan, 14, 2009

Facebook and other social media sites are great for staying in touch and sharing small and big moments with family, friends and assorted other connections. The key is making sure you're presenting the most appropriate profile possible to each "friend." If the flurry of publicity surrounding posting nude or inappropriate pictures on the Internet hasn't made you more cautious, maybe knowing that people like Bronk may be stalking you—some for monetary rewards and others because they are sexual predators—will dissuade you. Perhaps knowing that potential clients, your boss and even attorneys engaged in jury selection have been known to access your social media pages will discourage you from posting that picture of your bachelor party. A recent FindLaw survey found that 29 percent of social media users ages 18 to 34 have posted a photo, a comment or personal information that they fear could have repercussions at work.[11] Thankfully, legislation is addressing the need to restrict an employer's access to job applicants' and employees' personal data, but it is being done on a state-by-state basis so you will need to research your state's laws.

As far as potential jury selection, Philip K. Anthony, the CEO of a national trial consulting firm, DecisionQuest, suggests that certain people are too liberal to ever be picked for a criminal case. However, if they are working in an analytics field, they may be selected for an intellectual property case where their ability to analyze data and be

---

[11] Zukerberg, Randi, "Post More Baby Photos!", *Time*, Nov. 4, 2013 pg. 22

precise would be an asset.[12] Much of the data gathered to help in jury selection can be found on social media sites. Lawyers look at sites like Facebook, LinkedIn and Twitter to see how a jury member thinks. They then use this data to try to pick jurors who are sympathetic to their client or to disqualify an unsympathetic prospective juror. Also, after a verdict has been reached, what a juror reveals about the trial on these social media sites can potentially be used as a means for an appeal.[13]

> Legislation to restrict employers' access to applicants' and employees' personal online content continues its rapid expansion in 2014. Wisconsin and Tennessee became the 13th and 14th states to adopt a social media password protection law. The new laws prohibit an employer from requesting or requiring that applicants or employees disclose their passwords for personal Internet accounts.[14]

The victims of George Bronk all thought they had robust passwords, but he still managed to figure them out. His case illustrates the vulnerability of all Internet users. Whenever you access an online site, whether you are ordering a book, checking your bank balance, sending tweets or just browsing for new lamps, you are adding to your digital footprint. Behind the scenes, data aggregators and

---

[12] Stein, Joel, "12 Votes Down", *Time*, Sept. 16, 2013 pg. 60

[13] CNN News Analyst: Aug 8, 2013; CNN

[14] Gordon, Philip & Hwang, Joon, "Tennessee Joins The Growing List of States Limiting Employers' Access To Personal Online Content", *Mondaq*, May 14, 2014, http://www.mondaq.com/unitedstates/x/313366/employee+rights+labour+relations/ Tennessee+Joins+the+Growing+List+of+States+Limiting+Employers+Access+to+Per sonal+Online+Content

information brokers are compiling huge amounts of information about your personal preferences and habits, and they know your interests and hobbies, your financial transactions, your life events like marriages and divorces, and much, much more. They get this from cookies, public records, your online search results, the products you have purchased and the emails you open, to name a few. It is estimated that on average, they collect 1,500 pieces of unique personal information on each individual.[15] And I'd bet you never realized you were that interesting to someone!

The reason you are so interesting is that this information can be used for marketing and decision making. The average person receives four unsolicited emails per day as a result of the information that the data aggregators collect and sell to "Customer Intelligence Providers", companies who do targeted research around individual users and groups of users. After the data is analyzed, a company can then target advertisements and solicitations based on your preferences.

> The Chicago Tribune reported that "ENOVA International...analyzes more than two dozen data sources to determine, in less than 10 minutes, whether an applicant will qualify for one of its three-year, $10,000 loans. ....[C]ompanies find it easier to capture, store, crunch and share the data in ways that help their businesses serve customers, predict their behavior, innovate, improve productivity and cut costs...it includes blog posts, social-media feeds, GPS tracking data, online chat rooms, and most audio and video content."[16]

---

[15] Lin, Judy; "George Bronk Sentenced For Facebook Stalking", *Huffington Post*; July 22, 2011.

[16] Chicago Tribune, Business Section, Aug. 25, 2013

Over 500 million tweets are sent daily, more than doubling each year. What is said on Twitter and other social media sites is valuable to researchers, advertisers and campaign managers, but gathering those tweets present an ethical quandary…individual tweeters are not consenting to be part of any research. [17]

WHAT CAN YOU DO?

You have to realize that when using Facebook, MySpace, Twitter and other social media sites, nothing you put on them is truly private. Yes, you can control how users see or don't see your profile. But every time you 'like' a product or even look at a page, the company itself is taking note. This doesn't mean that someday Facebook will malevolently release your every click to the world. But it's also not your private diary, and what you do on the website is collected and cataloged. You should always keep that in mind when you're using a service.

Remember that even potential employers may review public parts of your footprint, such as your social media presence, when considering you for a job—just one more reason to be aware of what information is out there and to make sure it is accurate.

Parents need to monitor what images their children are presenting online because anything that might be perceived as suggestive or for mature audiences may attract undesirable attention including sexual predators. If your

---

[17] *Time Magazine;* Sept 9, 2013

child is under 13, the Children's Online Privacy Protection Act and Rule requires social networking websites to get parental consent before they collect, maintain or use a child's personal information. Keep the computer in a common area such as the den, family room or kitchen where you can regularly monitor your children when they are online and set time limits.

Recent updates make the Children's Online Privacy Protection Act (COPPA) more relevant in the social media and mobile phone age, and places some additional burdens on companies that target kids under 13. The rules went live over objections from industry groups that recently requested a postponement. Websites and phone apps that collect photos or geo-location data from children must now obtain express permission from parents, putting that data in the same category as kids' email or home addresses.

The new rules also make firms more responsible for data collection by third parties, a loophole that had been exploited by marketers in the past. Parents might not notice much change at first but some apps that kids use might begin requesting parental permissions via emails or other methods. Parents should make sure kids don't circumvent those rules by using a fake email address to grant themselves permission.[18]

---

[18] Sullivan, Bob, "New online child safety rules aim to protect kids on social media, smartphones", *NBC News*, Jul 1, 2013, http://www.nbcnews.com/business/consumer/new-online-child-safety-rules-aim-protect-kids-social-media-f6C10505412

> Facebook apologized for leaking contact information for an estimated six million users of the world's largest social network. But according to computer security experts, the site may be drastically underestimating the extent to which personal data was leaked, suggesting the number of Americans affected is indeed far higher. Further, many will never even know their data was compromised.[19]

Facebook has updated its privacy settings time and time again to make them more user friendly, so customizing your settings is a fairly straightforward procedure. It's an important one, too, since Facebook tends to automatically "opt" you in to new information sharing unless you go through and manually adjust the settings to the level of transparency you want.

If you subscribe to any social media, you must read their Statement of Rights and "opt out" of features you do not want. If you do not, you may find that all of your data is subject to being sold to a third-party vendor or used by the marketing arm of the social media site. Since they are the largest social network, we have provided an example of some of Facebook's Statement of Rights, which is similar to those of other social networks, at the end of this section

Facebook is not alone in selling your data. MySpace has had to agree, as part of a legal settlement with the FTC, to establish a comprehensive privacy program designed to protect consumers' information; they will be subjected to third-party audits of their privacy program for the next 20 years. The FTC claimed that MySpace shared personally

---

[19] http://www.techlicious.com/blog/experts-facebook-security-leak-more-extensive-than-site-is-admitting/

identifiable information with advertisers who could use MySpace's Friend ID to locate a user's profile, which included, in most instances, the user's full name as well as age, gender and profile picture.

MySpace also falsely certified that it complied with the U.S.-E.U. Safe Harbor Framework, according to the FTC, and the FTC accused Myspace of violating their own privacy policy, which stated they would not share users' personally identifiable information with third parties unless permission had been given to do so.

When it comes to advertising, Facebook hasn't changed its ways, but is, instead, trying to explain its practices and resolve previous ambiguity that upset some people so much that they sued the social network. In 2011, Facebook was accused of violating users' right to privacy by publicizing their "likes" in advertisements without asking them or compensating them. Since then, Facebook made changes to the two key documents that govern its service, in part to settle a two-year legal battle around its practice of using member data in advertisements. The social network has made updates, some of which have been court-ordered, to its Statement of Rights and Responsibilities and Data Use Policy legal documents to better inform members on how their data is used for advertising purposes and provide additional clarity on its data collection practices.

To sum it up, remember these five important tips for protecting yourself and your data on social media sites:

1. Don't be too personal. Keep most of your life private and think twice before posting information about yourself or your family.

2. Lock your phone. It may end up in the hands of strangers, giving access to your social accounts where they can target your friends using your profile as bait.

3. Use a unique password for each social media site and change your password often.

4. Choose your social network carefully. Evaluate the site that you plan to use and make sure you understand the privacy policy.

5. Talk to your children about social networking.

Privacy Software

Privacy software is built to protect the privacy of its users and typically works in conjunction with Internet usage to control or limit the amount of information made available to third-parties. The software can apply encryption or filtering of various kinds.

Privacy software can refer to two different types of protection. One type is protecting a user's Internet privacy from the World Wide Web. There are software products that will mask or hide a user's IP address from the outside world in order to protect the user from identity theft. The second type of protection is hiding or deleting the user's Internet traces that are left on their PC after they have been surfing the Internet. This software will erase all of the user's Internet traces and encrypt a user's traces so that others using their PC will not know where they have been surfing.

Even TechMedia Network, one of the companies that use data to tailor personalized purchase recommendations to technology consumers, says, "We must protect ourselves from hackers who want to steal identities, as well as from legitimate businesses who want to know our patterns so that they can advertise based on known interests. We could become indignant that it is now necessary to buy products to maintain privacy that we should never have lost. But surely a more useful response is the determination to defend now against inevitable attacks on our privacy."[20]

The top rated privacy software for 2014, according to TechMedia Network, is CyberScrub Privacy Suite, followed by Pareto Logic Privacy Control and WinSweeper. All three have excellent ratings. In order to know what to look for when you are evaluating privacy software, TechMedia Network recommends:[21]

1. While you are connected to the Internet, the software should maintain your privacy, and after your surfing session is over, it should erase evidence that might allow someone to reconstruct which sites you visited and what you did.

2. Privacy software should include browser cleaning, which removes data that accumulates in the address bar history, cookies, visited sites, downloads and

---

[20] TechMedia Network; privacy-software-review.toptenreviews.com
[21] TechMedia Network, ibid

favorites list. Other areas that require cleaning are the temporary Internet files and Windows system features such as the temporary files, recycle bin, computer history and clipboard. You might also consider file shredding and free-space wiping.

3. Will the product let you pick which cookies and files to keep and which to remove? You need a program that is easy to use and has software that is easy to program.

4. Consider support options and available hours for obtaining help from a help desk. Is there in-context help?

FACEBOOK'S STATEMENT OF RIGHTS

After a court settlement, Facebook's proposed Statement of Rights section on advertisements reads:

> You give us permission to use your name, and profile picture, content, and information in connection with commercial, sponsored, or related content (such as a brand you like) served or enhanced by us. This means, for example, that you permit a business or other entity to pay us to display your name and/or profile picture with your content or information, without any compensation to you. If you have selected a specific audience for your content or information, we will respect your choice when we use it. If you are under the age of eighteen (18), or under any other applicable age of majority, you represent that at least one of your parents or legal guardians has also agreed to the terms of this section (and the use of your name, profile picture, content, and information) on your behalf.[22]

---

[22] http://www.facebook.com/policies

The new advertising section in the revised data policy, meanwhile, is even more extensive and includes examples of how member data can be used along ads. Part of the rewritten section reads:

In addition to delivering relevant ads, Facebook sometimes pairs ads with social context, meaning stories about social actions that you or your friends have taken. For example, an ad for a sushi restaurant's Facebook Page may be paired with a News Feed story that one of your friends likes that page.

When you read the rest of the proposed terms of service, you'll find additional language changes meant to clarify what you can expect or not expect from your social-networking experience. The company now explains that if you want a third-party application you've connected to Facebook to delete your data, you'll have to go to the app-maker to make the request; in other words, Facebook isn't responsible. Facebook also explains that users are responsible for carrier data charges when using Facebook from their mobile devices.[23]

In addition, in the data policy the social network now makes it clear that it receives data on the type of device a person is using to run Facebook and includes more detail on the types of data, such as mobile phone number or operating system, that it receives from the devices members use to install Facebook apps or access the social network.

---

[23] http://www.facebook.com/legal/terms

ONLINE MARKETPLACES

Police in Chicago have labeled Craigslist crimes as "robbery by appointment" because criminals in the Windy City regularly use Craigslist to identify victims and have the luxury of scheduling their crimes. The most notorious crime led to an entire family being taken hostage and the father shot dead in front of his wife and children, who were also assaulted.[24]

In Craigslist's defense, millions of transactions have taken place safely using their service. It's sad to think that you can't trust anyone, but you don't want to be the next victim so it pays to be careful. Craigslist and other sites that act as online marketplaces might seem harmless—just a kind of online flea market—but you have to be wary. Whether you're selling a table or meeting a mate, reading between the lines is crucial to determining ahead of time if someone might be a bit iffy. When selling or buying something on Craigslist, protect yourself as much as possible. Always have a buddy with you as backup in case anyone weird shows up. Instead of giving your name and address to a total stranger, arrange to meet Craigslist buyers or sellers during the day in a public place. The right public place is somewhere that's not too crowded but has people around because you want people to notice if something goes wrong. And stick to the old adage, "If an ad seems too good to be true, it probably is."

---

[24] Chansanchai, Athima, "Rival links Craigslist to 12 deaths, 330 crimes in past year", *Today Tech*, Feb. 25, 2011, http://www.today.com/tech/rival-links-craigslist-12-deaths-330-crimes-past-year-124931

So everyone knows that Craigslist deals carry certain risks. Yet it's still difficult to get a big-picture perspective of both the scale and the general tenor of crime on Craigslist. We logged 74 different incidents occurring on Craigslist in 27 states and the District of Columbia within 30 days. Eleven of the incidents resulted in violence. Three of those resulted in death. Another eight carried a threat of violence. While the overall range of crimes that were committed was fairly wide, most tended to fall into a few distinct categories. Surprising to no one, the single most prevalent crime was robbery, attempted robbery, or assault. People arranged a meeting over Craigslist and then, during the meeting, one party would rob and/or assault the other.[25]

WHAT CAN YOU DO?

If you do have to give out your phone number, sign up for Gmail and get a free Google Voice number, which you can use to forward calls to your cell phone or landline. You'll be able to give this secondary number to someone you meet on Craigslist without revealing your primary contact info. Then, if something goes wrong, you'll be able to block them or just drop the Google number. It's an easy way to protect your privacy and your existing phone lines.

Google's own site says, "Google Voice isn't a phone service, but it lets you manage all of your phones. Google Voice works with mobile phones, desk phones, work phones, and VoIP lines. There's nothing to download, upload, or install, and you don't have to make or take calls using a computer. Google Voice will let you define which phones ring, based

---

[25] Sankin, Aaron, "Mapping of 30 Days of Craiglist Crimes", *DailyDot,* May 6, 2014, http://www.dailydot.com/crime/craigslist-crime-map/

on who's calling, and even let you listen in on voicemail before answering the call."[26]

Not a bad way to screen calls—not only for online selling, but also for managing those intrusive telemarketing calls.

---

[26] Google support, "About Google Voice", https://support.google.com/voice/answer/115061?hl=en

Chapter 2
Is My Car Spying On Me?

There was a time, not so long ago, when the idea of a talking car was confined to movies and TV programs. Now Siri uses positional and personal data to let you know where to find the closest pizza joint, where to locate gas on the interstate, and the best route to take home. While these are all wonderful applications of data, there is some not-so-wonderful intelligence your car gathers and provides to others. This chapter explores some of the ways your car gathers significant information about you and your habits.

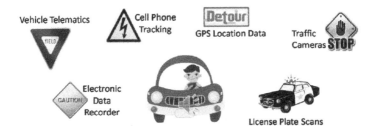

How Your Car Spies On You

LICENSE PLATE SCANS

Until articles started showing up in newspapers and magazines, very few people realized that their local police department might be keeping close track of where they go, who they see, and what businesses they frequent. For the average person, the concept behind license plate scans might seem like a good idea, since the police claim that once they load the license plate data into a state or national database, they can be on the lookout for stolen cars or people involved in criminal acts. And it *is* a good idea, but what about the rest of us who are not criminals and don't want dozens, and sometimes hundreds, of pictures of our license plates, along with the GPS co-ordinates that indicate where we were when the picture was taken, stored in some database indefinitely? The vast majority of the plates being scanned, estimated at 99 percent[27], can reveal things that innocent, law-abiding citizens might expect to remain private. Many police departments are collecting and storing location information about everyone who drives a car. Some police have defended this practice by arguing, essentially, that "you never know when or what we might need to solve a crime".[28]

License plate scanning occurs as police drive their cars in their normal course of duties. The scans are immediately matched against a database of known stolen vehicles. If a match is detected, a beeping noise or siren goes off inside the police car.[29] License plate scanning cameras can be mounted on the trunk or the hood of a police car, or they can be installed inconspicuously in the light bar on the roof of the car. In some cases, plate scans can be combined with other data to flesh out a sharper profile of a suspect. Even

[27] Sullivan, Mark "Plate Scanning, The Inside Story of a Cop Who Tracks Our Data", *CIO*, July 22, 2013

[28] "You can't hide from cops with license plate scanners" *USA Today*, Jul 18, 2013, www.usatoday.com

[29] Wikipedia, "Automatic number plate recognition", http://en.wikipedia.org/wiki/Automatic_number_plate_recognition

when police have only a partial scan of a license plate, historical scan data can reveal the full plate number, and eventually, the owner of the vehicle. Plate scans can yield more than just the number; the images often include a large portion of the car surrounding the license plate as well as a GPS tag of the exact location of the scan and a time stamp. All this information can be sent back to a database in milliseconds. Because the cameras are continually scanning, the same vehicles show up over and over again. When these scans are plotted on a map, individual license plate numbers can begin showing up in clusters revealing the places a person frequents. [30]

In the 1980s, London earned the dubious distinction of becoming the city with the most surveillance cameras in the world.[31] Mass license plate scanning became one of their techniques and was used as a way of keeping track of terrorists from the time they entered the city limits to the time they left. Law enforcement bodies around the world quickly saw the appeal of this and adopted the technology to find criminals and hunt down stolen vehicles. As plate scanning technology matured, it became a major law enforcement tool for finding criminals. By 2000, police in the United States were routinely using the technology. After 9/11, police departments nationwide suddenly had a lot more federal funding from the Department of Homeland

---

[30] "CIO; Plate Scanning: The Inside Story of a Cop Who Tracks our Data"; By Mark Sullivan Mon, July 22, 2013 inShare2; *IDG News Service*

[31] Barrett, David, "One surveillance camera for every 11 people in Britian", *The Telegraph*, Jul 10, 2013

Security for all kinds of surveillance gear including license plate scanning devices.

As far back as 2007, the American Civil Liberties Union (ACLU) was reporting that "the government is compiling some data, not for the purposes of any kind of immediate scrutiny, but in order to build up a sea of information to have on hand just in case analysts want to 'swim through it' on a particular investigation. That would let them skip the trouble of having to go to a judge and request approval for specific data—in essence, a shortcut around the Constitution. It is now clear that this is exactly what the NSA is doing with phone records, and who knows what other kinds of records—and what some local police departments are doing with license plate data. We now have technologies that enable the creation of very detailed data on our activities. Those technologies are only going to get more powerful and more pervasive. We need to make a choice as a society about the extent to which we want to allow the government to store up that data so that it has the power to hit 'rewind' on everybody's lives."[32]

"They have really ramped up the number of cameras in the last few years. And they're using longer retention times for the data." says Electronic Freedom Foundation staff attorney Jennifer Lynch.[33]

---

[32] Stanley, Jay, "From the NSA to License Plate Readers, Are we to Have a 'Collect it All' Society?", *ACLU*, Jul 26, 2013; https://www.aclu.org/blog/national-security-technology-and-liberty-free-speech/nsa-license-plate-readers-are-we-have

[33] Lynch, Jennifer, "National License Plate Recognition Database: What It Is and Why It's a Bad Idea", *Electronic Frontier Foundation*, Feb. 19, 2013;

How do license plate scan readers, referred to by the acronym LPSR, work? Mounted on police cruisers and using an array of high-speed cameras snapping pictures, these systems are designed to capture up to 2,000 plates per minute, even at high speeds and in difficult driving conditions. The date, time, license plate number, and GPS coordinates are stored each time a license plate is read. The data is then loaded onto a server where it is compared to plate numbers of all known stolen vehicles in the United States. If the system finds a plate that is in the stolen car database, it alerts the officer.[34] While this is a new and effective way for the police to help fight crime, many people are leery of a new technology that has the potential to scan a million license plates a year with a single device.

> License plate reader systems allow anyone with access to these systems to track his boss, his ex-wife, his romantic or workplace rivals, friends, enemies, neighbors, or family. An agent could target the owners of vehicles parked at political meetings, gay bars, gun stores, or abortion clinics.[35]

Right now there are few standards or written policies, and state legislatures are just getting around to thinking about restricting the use of scanners or enacting laws for disposing of license plate pictures after a set amount of time. Under consideration are policies such as prohibiting use of camera

---

https://www.eff.org/deeplinks/2014/02/national-license-plate-recognition-database-what-it-and-why-its-bad-idea

[34] Hall, Cristina "License-plate scanners on cop cars: Crime-fighting tool or invasion of privacy?", *Detroit Free Press*, Nov. 1, 2013

[35] American Civil Liberties Union, "You are Being Tracked", *ACLU*, Jul, 2013, https://www.aclu.org/files/assets/071613-aclu-alprreport-opt-v05.pdf

scanners to intimidate or harass; to infringe on free speech; or to conduct discriminatory surveillance based on race, gender, sexual orientation, disability, or other protected characteristics.

As the technology spreads, the ACLU has called for the adoption of legislation and law enforcement policies adhering to the following principles:

1. License plate readers may be used by law enforcement agencies only to investigate those license plates that match stolen cars and in other circumstances in which law enforcement agents reasonably believe that the plate data are relevant to an ongoing criminal investigation.

2. The government must not store data about innocent people for any lengthy period. Unless plate data has been flagged, retention periods should be measured in days or weeks, not months, and certainly not years.

3. People should be able to find out if plate data of vehicles registered to them are contained in a law enforcement agency's database.

4. Law enforcement agencies should not share license plate reader data with third parties that do not follow proper retention and access principles. They should also be transparent regarding with whom they share license plate reader data.

5. Any entity that uses license plate readers should be required to report its usage publicly on at least an annual basis.[36]

The Associated Press reported that plainclothes NYPD officers used readers to scan license plates of people worshipping at a mosque in 2006 and 2007, under a program that was partially funded by a federal drug enforcement grant.[37]

In Washington, D.C., nearly every block is captured by one of the more than 250 cameras scanning over 1,800 images per minute. In Los Angeles, more than two dozen different law enforcement agencies operate license plate readers to collect over 160 million data points. This surveillance is untargeted, recording the movements of any car that passes by. In cities that have become partners in the FBI's Joint Terrorism Task Force, or which have entered into another data-sharing agreement, this location information is at the fingertips of those federal agents.

The Chicago Tribune revealed that additional installations of stop sign enforcement cameras are being tested in Washington, D.C., Chicago and cities in California.[38] Just one more way to capture license plate information in our surveillance society. Police argue that since license plates are

36 ACLU Report, "You Are Being Tracked", *American Civil Liberties Union*, https://www.aclu.org/alpr

37 Goldman, Adam & Apuzzo, Matt, "With cameras, informants, NYPD eyed mosques", *Associated Press*, Feb. 23, 2013

38 Zorn, Eric, "Opinion", *Chicago Tribune*, September 15, 2013

mounted on the outside of the car, they are not protected and can be photographed by anyone. They also contend that stationary plate-scanning cameras have been used for some time at the sides of busy thoroughfares or at state or national border crossings. What authorities haven't disclosed is that images of drivers captured by police cameras at stoplights can be matched with plates to attach a face with a plate number.

WHAT CAN YOU DO?

It is encouraging to see that articles are being written to alert the public to this new threat on personal data. Until laws are enacted, however, one thing you can do is to ask your local police department if they use license plate scanners --and if they do—how long the records are kept. You can also ask what type of policies your local law enforcement agencies have enacted to prevent discriminatory surveillance.

Once it is known that people are asking questions, it will hasten the enactment and enforcement of standards and policies. While most police departments have rules about how the scan data can be used, there's no way to know how and if the rules are actually enforced. And these rules vary widely from department to department. One police department, documented in an ACLU report, says the use of the scan database is limited "only by the officer's imagination."

A number of organizations and individuals filed amicus briefs in September 2013 in support of the ACLU's constitutional challenge to the government's collection of the call records of virtually everyone in the United States.

An amicus brief is a document filed by a party that is not involved in a particular litigation but that is allowed by the court to advise it on a matter of law directly affecting the litigation. If you feel you are being unfairly targeted, you can file a FOIA (Freedom of Information Act) request for patrol scans on your vehicle. You can also call or write your state or local government representatives and ask them to consider legislation that will balance legitimate use of license plate scans for crime prevention or criminal apprehension with the people's expectation of privacy.

There are a range of groups joining the protest against mass government surveillance, not to mention the bipartisan storm that has swept Congress since the recent NSA disclosures. Americans from every political party think that the government's dragnet surveillance practices are offensive. The FBI has had some of its domestic surveillance activities curtailed (but not eliminated) in the wake of the landmark 2013 Supreme Court decision in United States v. Jones. In Jones, a unanimous court held that federal agents must get a warrant to attach a GPS device to a car to track a suspect for long periods of time, which was the FBI's previous go-to surveillance technique. This ruling, however, did not include the tracking of cars and their occupants by cell phone transmissions and/or license plate scans.[39]

---

[39] Sacks, Mike, "Warrantless GPS Tracking Unconstitutional, Supreme Court Rules", *Huffington Post,* Jan 23, 2012

TELEMATIC DEVICES

The police aren't the only ones collecting your data. Insurance companies have a new gimmick—a telematic device for your car. Using catchy names such as "Snapshot" and "Drivewise," insurance companies are asking drivers to install a device that would monitor their driving habits in exchange for lower rates. In a recent survey, the *Chicago Tribune* reports that 40 percent of drivers said "no way in hell."[40]

The recent disclosure that the NSA routinely violated individual privacy has had the effect of keeping people from being sold on the benefits of telematic monitoring, yet insurance companies are betting that at least six million of the devices will be installed each year. Dave Pratt, Progressive's general manager for usage-based insurance, acknowledged that "car devices are a sensitive issue and motorists deserve to know what data is being collected, how it's being used and with whom it is being shared."[41]

The National Association of Insurance Commissioners said that it expects 20 percent of insurance companies will incorporate some form of telematics within a few years. A big factor is that today's younger generations are more open to sharing personal information on social media and therefore will be less concerned about privacy issues involving telematics.

---

[40] Yerek, Becky, "Motorists tap the brakes on installing data devices for insurance companies", *Chicago Tribune*, Sep 15, 2013

[41] Yerek, Becky, Ibid

Insurance companies see telematics as good for both underwriting and claims. Telematics promise to fundamentally change auto insurance pricing because the information contained in black box technologies measures risk characteristics in the form of actual driving behavior data (miles traveled, average speed, and much more), in contrast to traditional rating factors such as miles driven to work, age, and other factors. Telematics data will likely be used to build next-generation scoring models and analytics, too.

> We are already going down a slippery slope when it comes to personal privacy and liberty. While I recognize driving is a privilege, not a right, I still think this is going too far. There are all sorts of privacy threats floating around out there pertaining to your vehicle and your travel habits. You just wait and see where this leads. Over time this 'black box' will be mandated to capture more and more data that WILL BE USED AGAINST YOU, you can count on that.[42]

Pinnacle Actuarial Resources Inc. shared results of an analysis of about 2,000 sentiments expressed on Twitter about Progressive's Snapshot telematics device over a recent ten-month period. People not using Snapshot were the most negative. Their biggest concern was privacy, particularly the belief that insurers might track their locations despite assurances that the technology monitors only mileage, braking, and other driving habits. The tweets were nearly evenly split between people who weren't using Snapshot and those who were in various stages of using it. In tone, 55

---

[42] Anonymous Tweet recorded on Exhaust Notes, May 15, 2012

percent were negative, 26 percent were positive and 19 percent were neutral.[43]

Unfortunately you may have an electronic data recorder in your vehicle right now. You don't even have to agree to install a "driving behavior" device. Electronic Data Recorders (EDRs) collect raw vehicle data and overlay this information with geographic information and system mapping data such as road type and speed limits. As the cost of enabling technologies such as Wi-Fi, GPS, Bluetooth, 3-axis accelerometers, and mobile broadband communications have fallen—and as original equipment manufacturers are increasingly embedding telematics in vehicles—the result is that telematics are now in an estimated 70 percent of post-2011 vehicles. [44]

These electronic data recorders are of primary interest to insurance companies because of the potential information they can get from them in case of an accident. Greg Horn, former VP at GMAC Insurance says "Most EDRs gather data during a full frontal collision that causes visible damage to the vehicle, when there is sufficient damage to deploy the air bags. Potholes, curb hits, and the like do not generate data of interest to most EDRs at the moment, but as vehicles become more sophisticated and costly to repair, these seemingly minor bumps and bruises can set off a significant claims event. Side-impact air bags and rollover sensors collect more information, and these advancements

[43] Yerek, Becky, Ibid

[44] Horn, Greg, "Vehicle Telematics Is the black box really a Pandora's box for insurers?", *Claims Management*, Feb. 7, 2012

are making their way into more vehicles." [45] These black boxes, after being deployed by a significant bump, will record the date and time when triggered, the vehicle speed, engine speed, steering angle, throttle position, braking status, force of impact, seat belt status, and airbag deployment. Thank goodness they cannot tell who was driving and where—yet!

Monitoring of fleet vehicles has shown that vehicles can easily be tracked as to location, movement and behavior. Using a combination of a GPS and an EDR, the data is then turned into information on a visual display on computerized mapping software. Even speed can be controlled by adaptive cruise control.

While making EDR data usable can be a real challenge, some vehicle manufacturers have licensed third parties to develop tools to download data from an EDR. Today, few— including most professional accident reconstructionists— can retrieve EDR data. The data retrieval requirements are different from service technicians' diagnostic equipment, too. The challenge for insurance adjusters is that some manufacturers have ensured that only their own engineers can retrieve the data which limits how much data the insurance companies can realistically collect.

WHAT CAN YOU DO?

In the event of an accident, how the data on the event data recorder (EDR) is used is not standard across states nor

---

[45] Horn, Greg, Ibid

across insurance companies. Some carriers assert in their policy contracts that the insured agrees to data collection from such devices under an "Agreement to Cooperate" clause. However, some states have statutes that nullify these clauses, and there is plenty of potential for litigation. Currently, several states have statutes that regulate who owns the data from a car's EDR and who can gain access to it. In many states, a warrant is required to access the data without the owner's consent. But as with any law, exceptions exist, and a court order can be used to force a car owner to hand over black box data in legal proceedings. Insurers need a state-specific handling procedure to identify a potential vehicle with an EDR, and the insured needs to know if their insurance company claims it has a right to their car's data recorder.

Courts can subpoena EDR data through court orders, and some states collect data under their existing laws governing crash investigations. There is a body of court cases where EDR data has been accepted in the proceedings. Also, there is a loophole as to who owns the data. When a car is totaled, it becomes the property of the driver's auto insurance company. The insurer then owns the EDR and could possibly use it as evidence in a court case.[46]

Federal legislation is pending that would institute a legal standard nationwide. The proposed law would allow only emergency personnel, such as police, firefighters, and paramedics, access to the data without a court order if it helps them better respond to an accident. As with all

---

[46] http://www.nsl.org

legislation, you should make your voice heard by writing to your elected officials if you feel "black boxes" are an invasion of your personal privacy.

THE LITTLE BLACK BOX AND TAXES

According to a *Chicago Tribune* report from Oct. 27, 2013, another threat to personal data looms as officials ponder the use of EDR devices as a way to supplement falling motor vehicle taxes based on how far each person drives. Unlikely as it seems, Libertarians have joined environmental groups in lobbying for a system where the government would use the boxes to keep track of how many miles you drive and possibly where you drive. Naturally the ACLU is against this proposal, but several states are exploring how they can charge drivers for every mile they drive. The environmentalists think fees could be staggered to help reduce congestion and greenhouse gases, and the Libertarians feel people could choose how much they want to drive if they have to pay for each mile. They feel it would be a more direct tax. There are already test markets up and running in Oregon, Nevada, and California, but there are major concerns about "big brother."

There are some positive aspects to having a black box in every car. In New York City, transportation officials are thinking of a taxing device that could pay parking meters and toll road fees, provide "pay as you drive" auto insurance, and collect data that could re-route traffic from congested areas. But at what cost to personal freedom? The automobile gave people the ability to escape the narrow confines of their immediate area by letting them travel when and where they choose. Now that freedom may be restricted in ways not even contemplated by today's mobile society.

WHAT CAN YOU DO?

Many people feel that the problem of falling fuel taxes could be addressed with a less radical approach than monitoring every driver and how much he drives. Raising gas taxes has been suggested, as have more toll roads that could pay for themselves. Once again, the best way to stop any new legislation is to write or telephone your congressman and voice your opinion. As much as we sometimes think our officials don't care about the "average" person, they care about your vote—so make it count. Monitoring drivers will only mean that more of your personal information is collected and shared with many more agencies.

CAN MY CAR'S OPERATING SYSTEM BE HACKED?

Of course it can. Anything that uses a computer to operate it or any of its systems can be hacked, but the potential for harm has been largely swept under the rug by car manufacturers. The fact that criminals can either remotely or directly take control of your car from their laptop was demonstrated at Defcon in 2013 by security engineers from Twitter and IOActive, a Seattle consultancy company. Much of this work had been funded by the Pentagon (for what purpose we can only guess), and tests have shown that attack software can kill power steering, slam on brakes, blast horns, and disrupt GPS and odometers.[47] If hackers can do all that, you can be sure that they can also gather data from various automobile functions and use it to flesh out your profile—or, in extreme cases, for blackmail purposes.

At the Black Hat Asia security conference in Singapore in March 2014, Spanish security researchers Javier Vazquez-Vidal and Alberto Garcia Illera presented a small gadget they built for less than $20 that can be physically connected to a car's internal network to inject malicious commands affecting everything from its windows and headlights to its steering and brakes. Their tool, which is about three-quarters the size of an iPhone, attaches via four wires to the Controller Area Network bus of a vehicle, drawing power from the car's electrical system and waiting to relay wireless commands sent remotely from an attacker's computer. They call their creation the CAN Hacking Tool, or CHT.[48]

Troels Oerting, the director of the Europe's Cybercrime Centre, a body within the European Union's law enforcement agency Europol, told CNBC that the potential for in-car technology to be hacked and used for organized crime, revenge, profit, and competitive advantage was great.

"We are very concerned about the direction of car hacking," Oerting told CNBC. "Everyone [in the car industry] wants to make cars more helpful—for them to help with steering, parking, breaking, and even driving—but if you do this, the

---

[47] Digital Carjackers; *Forbes*; August 12, 2013 pgs. 45-47

[48] Greenberg, Andy, "This iPhone-Sized Device Can Hack A Car, Researchers Plan To Demonstrate" *Forbes*, Feb. 5, 2014

downside is that someone will try to use this to their advantage and for criminals, this would generally be for profit or revenge."[49] Scary stuff, and although the car companies are assuring the public that they are aware of the threats and are working to make their cars' computer systems "hacker-proof", there is no guarantee. Oerting stated that "The best we can do right now is to make consumers aware of the downside to technological developments, and to make people able to drive using this technology without fear every five seconds that your car will be taken over."[50]

ACCEPT THE REALITY

So in answer to the question posed at the beginning of this chapter, yes, your car is spying on you. But why be surprised? As you read through the chapters of this book you will find that your phone, your computer, your credit card company, your social media chat room, and even that friendly merchant you do business with in your own home town, are all gathering and selling your personal data. Our best salvation may be that consumers are getting wise to these tactics and are pushing back.

---

[49] "Car hacking: The next global cybercrime?" Friday, 18 Oct 2013, Holly Ellyatt, Assistant Producer, CNBC.com

[50] CNBC, Ibid

Chapter 3

Cards—Know When to Hold 'Em, Know When to Fold 'Em

T.J. Maxx's data breach that exposed the payment information of thousands of customers in 2007 resulted in $150 million in fraud losses, and much of it was pulled directly from customers' bank accounts. Although credit card users got their accounts straightened out and new cards were in the mail within a few days, the case created major problems for debit card holders, who waited an average of two to three months to get reimbursed.[51]

CREDIT CARDS

Credit card fraud is a wide-ranging term for theft and fraud committed using a credit or debit card to obtain fraudulent funds in a transaction. Credit card fraud is an adjunct to identity theft and is a real problem around the world, but the legal selling of credit card information by banks and other financial institutions is just as alarming.

While some identity thieves focus on getting your credit cards and maxing them out before you even realize they're missing, an increasing number are using one piece of information about you—often a credit card number—in order to steal your entire identity. Though many folks worry

---

[51] Bell, Clase, "4 risky places to swipe your debit card", Bankrate.com; http://www.bankrate.com/finance/checking/risky-places-swipe-debit-card-1.aspx

about keeping their credit card information secure when shopping online, the top methods that identity thieves use to steal personal data are still low-tech, according to Justin Yurek, president of ID Watchdog, an identity theft-monitoring firm. "Watch your personal documents, be careful to whom you give out your data over the phone, and be careful of mail theft," he says. [52]

Credit Card Fraud

Most people have more than one credit card, and having a half dozen is not uncommon. After all, all the major retailers entice you to sign up for their store credit cards by giving you 10-20 percent off the first purchase and the promise that you will receive "special" offers from them during the year. Many credit cards offer one-time bonuses of airline miles, special treatment as a "preferred customer" or no-interest for a period of time—all of which are hard to resist.

Provisions in the Gramm-Leach-Biley Act of 1999, also called the Federal Services Modernization Act, require every financial institution to annually notify all customers, in

---

[52] Rogak, Lisa, "10 things you should know about identity theft", *CreditCards.com*, http://www.creditcards.com/credit-card-news/help/10-things-you-should-know-about-identity-theft-6000.php

writing, of that organization's privacy policy. The purpose of the privacy provision of this act is to curtail the ability of third parties to obtain nonpublic personal information regarding individuals who purchase financial products like credit cards and/or services from financial institutions.

But how many of us read the fine print when we sign up for credit cards? I know I didn't, and until I started researching privacy policies for this book, I would typically take the privacy policy when it came in the mail, and pitch it into the wastebasket. Who wants to take the time to read pages of legal terms about privacy? There are laws against giving out our social security number or other sensitive information, aren't there? Look at this notice and decide for yourself.

> The types of personal information we collect and <u>share</u> depend on the product or service you have with us. This information can include:
>
> 1. Social security number and income
> 2. Account balances and credit history
> 3. Account transactions and credit card or other debt

Who sent this notice? Not a government agency, but Capital One when I applied for a Best Buy credit card. Lured by the promise of 10 percent off an expensive television, I thought, "What the heck? I'll get their credit card and then pay it off right away and probably never use it again." Little did I know how Capital One was going to share my personal information, nor how little I could do to limit that sharing. Also in the notice was the chilling statement that they would begin sharing my data in 30 days, and even if I was *no longer their customer*, they could continue to share my information.

Here are some ways they could share my data and what they said I could do—or not do—to stop them:[53]

Type of Information Sharing by Capital One for Best Buy	Can I limit sharing?
Credit bureaus	NO
Legal investigations	NO
Offer products and services to you	NO
Share with affiliates information about your experiences	NO
Information about your creditworthiness	YES
Joint marketing with other financial companies	NO
For our affiliates to market to you	YES
For our nonaffiliates to market to you	YES

Financial institutions aren't the only ones sharing our information. Here are some excerpts from Verizon's Privacy Policy, which covers what they call CPNI (Customer Proprietary Network Information):[54]

> We will share CPNI among our affiliates and parent companies and their subsidiaries so that they may market communications-related products and services to you and for making mobile ads you see more relevant. Although we will not identify you personally, we will use consumer information about your use of VERIZON products and services such as addresses of websites you visit when using our wireless service. Using certain consumer information (such as your demographics, device type and language preference) and the postal address we have for you, we will determine if you fit into an audience an advertiser is trying to reach. For example, a local restaurant may want to advertise only to people who live within 50 miles; and we might help deliver that ad on a website without sharing information that identifies you personally.[55]

---

[53] Best Buy Privacy Statement, Capital One Best Buy credit card notice

[54] Verizon http://www.verizon.com/about/privacy/policy/

[55] Verizon, Ibid

Okay, I guess that explains why I keep getting offers for pre-approved credit cards and from Groupon, Travelzoo and others for discounts to restaurants.

If you receive applications for "pre-approved" credit cards in the mail but discard them without tearing up the enclosed materials, criminals may retrieve them and try to activate the cards for their use without your knowledge. (Some credit card companies, when sending credit cards, have adopted security measures that allow a card recipient to activate the card only from his or her home telephone number, but this is not yet a universal practice.) Also, if your mail is delivered to a place where others have ready access to it, criminals may simply intercept and redirect your mail to another location.

With enough identifying information about an individual, a criminal can take over that individual's identity to conduct a wide range of crimes: for example, false applications for loans and credit cards, fraudulent withdrawals from bank accounts, fraudulent use of telephone calling cards, or obtaining other goods or privileges which the criminal might be denied if he were to use his real name. If the criminal takes steps to ensure that bills for the falsely obtained credit cards, or bank statements showing the unauthorized withdrawals are sent to an address other than the victim's, the victim may not become aware of what is happening until the criminal has already inflicted substantial damage on the victim's assets, credit, and reputation.[56]

DEBIT CARDS

Using a debit card seems like a great idea for the simple reason that you won't have the clerk at the local gas station ask for your phone number, driver's license, or other private information before he will accept your personal check, and you don't have to feel self-conscious at the grocery store when five people with full shopping baskets are glaring at you for holding up the line while you fumble for your checkbook. However, by using your debit card frequently, you may be giving crooks a direct line to your bank account.

Debit cards might look the same as credit cards, but they have a big difference. With a credit card you can look at your statement and decline any false charges and not pay the bill. With a debit card, the money is drawn directly from your checking account with no intermediary such as your credit card company. You don't have the same account monitoring as credit cards because transactions are processed through a different network, which only relies on your transaction history with that specific bank, not the entire Visa or Master Card system. And even though there are consumer protection laws that protect you from liability, it can be weeks before the money is restored to your

---

[56] U.S. Department of Justice, "Identity Theft and Identity Fraud", http://www.justice.gov/criminal/fraud/websites/idtheft.html

account. In the meantime, you do not have your funds to pay bills or draw upon for cash.

Using your debit card for online transactions is very risky because the card information is susceptible to being stolen at so many points. The consumer could have malware on their computer, so it could be at their end that the data is compromised. It could be an online attack where somebody is eavesdropping on their communications via the wireless network or at the other end when that data goes into the merchant's database. Aside from the potential for hacking at many different points in a transaction, a fundamental problem with using debit cards online is that it's impossible to know who is handling your information.

Restaurants have two problem areas with card transactions, first because it is easy for the server to steal your information when he takes your card to another location to process it, and second it is also easy to leave your card behind when he brings it back. Usually the card is laid on the table in a small binder, and if you are talking or not paying attention, you could walk away without your card. In Europe, they have addressed this by requiring, by law, that credit cards never leave the owner's sight. They process restaurant transactions at the table.

Even take-out restaurants can present a problem. Using debit cards to order delivery can be risky because pizza and other take-out restaurants like to keep customer payment information on file to speed up order taking. That may make future orders more convenient, but small businesses rarely take the steps necessary to safeguard payment information.

Do you really want the kid who works the register to have your debit or credit card information?

Experts recommend checking your accounts every few days, so using as few cards as possible makes sense since the more cards you carry, the more you have to check. Also, the more cards you have, the greater the chance of forgetting to retrieve it after a transaction.

Many people I know could not live without their ATM. They use it almost every day and seem to have the notion that carrying a debit card is safer than having cash in their wallets. Plus, the ATM allows them to deposit checks and retrieve their account balance 24 hours a day, 7 days a week. The problem is that identity thieves work 24/7 too, and have found ways to skim the information from your card. Skimming is the practice of capturing a bank customer's card information by running it through a machine that reads the card's magnetic strip. Those machines are often placed over the real card slots at ATMs and other card terminals. The keypads may show no sign of manipulation because the "bugging" device is on the inside of the keypad. Typically, these types of devices still transmit customer data to the bank, but they also capture personal information from the card and the card holder's PIN number.

Outdoor ATMs are among the most dangerous places to use a debit card because outdoor ATMs present a perfect opportunity for thieves to skim users' debit cards. You are much safer using an ATM inside a retail outlet or in other high-trafficked, well-lit place. Any transaction you do outdoors at an open ATM is going to expose you to higher risk because a thief has the ability to add skimming devices to it, position cameras on it, or position themselves in a way where they could watch it.[57]

WHAT CAN YOU DO?

Frank Abagnale, a security expert with PrivacyGuard, offers these tips:[58]

1. Review your credit and debit card accounts frequently so you can spot suspicious activity right away.

2. Do not trust keypads if they don't look quite right. Tampering by inexperienced criminals can sometimes be obvious. Make certain the keypad is firmly attached to the counter or console.

3. Protect your PIN by covering the keypad with your hand and do not use ATMs where you know there is a security camera positioned behind you.

Privacy concerns are providing the impetus for credit card companies to provide higher-security cards. The revelations about the National Security Agency spying, the many recent data breaches, high-profile data losses and the realization that data brokers are collecting huge amounts of data have

---

[57] McGoey, Chris, Security Expert, Quoted in *Wells Fargo Community,* Jan. 31, 2014, https://www.wellsfargocommunity.com/thread/3947

[58] Abengale, Frank, "Frank's Tips for Protecting Your Credit", Privacy Guard, www.privacyguard.com

heightened privacy concerns. The public does not believe that business or the government adequately protect consumer data.

To counteract those perceptions, Visa, MasterCard and other large credit card companies are mandating that credit card issuers must embed EMV chips, by October 2015 or they will be held responsible for the cost of any fraudulent in-person transactions due to counterfeit or stolen credit cards.

EMV stands for Europay, MasterCard and Visa and is the new global standards for credit cards. EMV chips have microprocessors embedded in them and are said to make counterfeiting cards virtually impossible. Most banks will be issuing credit cards with EMV chips before the coming liability shift in October 2015.

Businesses such as restaurants, where a server or clerk usually handles the card, will have to update procedures, retrain staff and validate their new approach with their payment processor. In addition, organizations may need to expand their wireless network to accommodate portable card readers.[59] This shift will cost businesses some extra money but the public will be better protected from credit card fraud.

---

[59] Perkins, Bart, "Forget the Cost, More Secure Cards are an Opportunity", *Computerworld*, Jun 17, 2014, http://www.computerworld.com/s/article/9249157/ Bart_Perkins_Forget_the_expense_more_secure_credit_cards_are_an_opportunity? taxonomyId=17&pageNumber=2

Chapter 4

Marketing to the Masses

Epsilon is the leading source of marketing data. We have information on more than 250 million consumers and 120 million business contacts, and we specialize in providing marketers with the clearest 360-degree view of their customer's lifestyles, attitudes and behaviors. It's this information that gives you the insight and the know-how you need for better campaign performance.[60]

TRACKING PURCHASES

The Wall Street Journal conducted a study that found that the nation's 50 top websites installed, on average, 64 pieces of tracking technology onto the computers of visitors, usually with no warning. A dozen sites each installed more than a hundred (the nonprofit Wikipedia installed none). Tracking isn't new, but the technology is growing so powerful and ubiquitous that even some of America's biggest sites say they were unaware, until informed by the *Journal*, that they were installing intrusive files on visitors' computers. Tracking companies sometimes hide their files within free software offered to websites or hide them within other tracking files or advertisements. When this happens,

---

[60] Epison Marketing Advertisement, http://www.epsilon.com/solutions/product-solutions/data

websites aren't always aware that they're installing the files on visitors' computers. Tracking technology is getting smarter and more intrusive; new tools scan in real time what people are doing on a Web page, then instantly assess location, income, shopping interests and even medical conditions. Some tools surreptitiously re-spawn themselves even after users try to delete them.[61]

United States businesses have more data stored per company than the U.S. Library of Congress. There is a lot of information out there about every one of us; it is sold on a daily basis to marketing firms so that big businesses can come up with relentless and targeted advertising campaigns. If you buy a bedspread from J.C. Penney with your credit card, you can probably expect a flood of mail order catalogs from places such as The Company Store, Sears and Bed Bath & Beyond in the next few months.

The typical information brokers sell to marketing agencies are names, addresses, contact information, age, race, occupation and education level. They also collect and sell lists of people who are experiencing life events such as getting married, having a baby, buying a home or getting divorced.

They also have data about many of the purchases you make or the hobbies you pursue, the places you travel (and how often) and the type of car you bought last year.

---

[61] Angwin, Julia "The New Goldmine, Your Personal Data and Tracking Online", *The Wall Street Journal*, July 30, 2010

Where are they getting all this info? The stores where you shop sell it to them. Datalogix, for instance, which collects information from store loyalty cards, says it has information on more than $1 trillion in consumer spending "across 1400+ leading brands." It doesn't say which ones because data companies usually refuse to say exactly which companies sell them information, citing competitive reasons. And retailers also don't make it easy for you to find out if they're selling your information.[62]

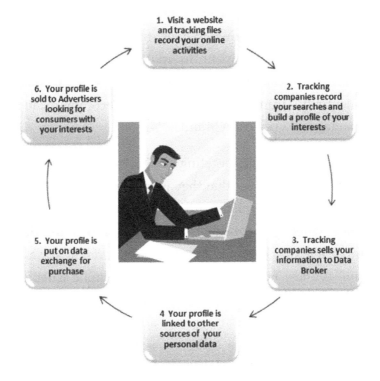

1. Visit a website and tracking files record your online activities

2. Tracking companies record your searches and build a profile of your interests

3. Tracking companies sells your information to Data Broker

4 Your profile is linked to other sources of your personal data

5. Your profile is put on data exchange for purchase

6. Your profile is sold to Advertisers looking for consumers with your interests

Stealing Your Online Data

---

[62] Beckett, Lois, "Everything We Know About Data Brokers Know About You", *Propublica.org*, September 13, 2013, https://www.propublica.org/article/everything-we-know-about-what-data-brokers-know-about-you

By now, many people are used to the way advertisements follow them around the Web—how the chair they clicked on here keeps popping up there. Annoying, but advertisers have come to regard this technique, called retargeting, as a very effective way of reaching their target audience.

Online marketing companies are already focusing on the next generation of targeted advertising—one that collects and analyzes vast streams of data from social media, credit card histories and Web habits. That information helps to create ads that are increasingly personalized and nuanced. Often, these ads are shown to consumers in real time based on what they do moment to moment. The amount of information available to advertisers has increased exponentially, from credit card and telecommunications companies and even from brands.

Instead of using old retargeting methods, such as showing someone an ad for a car that they just viewed online, brands are using new technologies to help them decide, often in advance, whether a consumer should be shown an ad, for example, a luxury car or an inexpensive car, or any car at all. In milliseconds, fast technologies can determine whether a person is in the market for a new car or has bought a car recently, yielding different types of ads. One ad could focus on a new vehicle that a company is trying to promote to energy-conscious drivers, while another might focus on accessories for the car. [63]

---

[63] Vega, Tanzina "New Ways Marketers Are Manipulating Data to Influence You", *New York Times* 6/20/13 pg F2

A value is assigned to a consumer, and how much the advertiser is willing to spend on that consumer can be based on myriad factors including whether and how that consumer uses social media, recent purchases and Web sites visited. If a consumer has a 20 percent chance of making a $100 purchase, that consumer could be valued at a certain level; conversely, if that person's dollar value is lower than the cost of marketing, an advertiser may opt not to show an ad to that person.

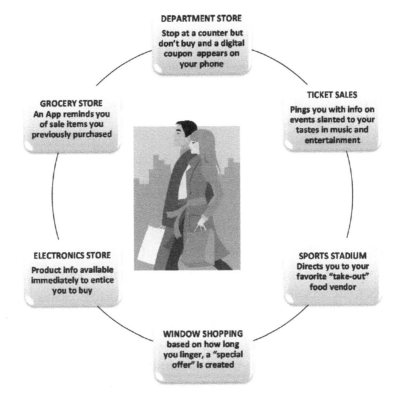

How Retailers Can Use Your Personal Information to "Upsell"

Grouping users by type is not new, but with increasingly large sets of data, the process is increasing in precision and gives brands a "feedback loop" with consumers so they know which ads are most effective with which consumers. Social media companies work with advertisers to help segment users based on what they are posting. The information gathered from comments posted about a brand or product on online retailers' websites, as well as comments gathered from social media, has created real-time focus groups and is an easy way for companies to compare their brand to those of their competitors.

> The rewards for being in the data brokerage industry are too great. It's obvious that companies are hungry to use data to inform their marketing campaigns. Data brokerage is booming. That's why Facebook keeps tightening alliances with three of the largest data brokers in the U.S., Datalogix, Acxiom, and Epsilon. It's more the fact that we aren't told when and where our data is collected, and that most people don't realize the extreme reach of these companies, that's so troubling.[64]

For example, Proclivity Media developed a proprietary technology based on the premise that every person has a constantly changing economic value in relation to any item in the world which could be computed in real time to optimize sales for a broad array of industries such as commerce, travel, education, non-profit and politics. The Proclivity Media technology platform drives sales for companies by rapidly ingesting and scoring an ever-increasing volume of data about their products and consumers to predict what consumers are likely to buy,

[64] Knibbs, Kate, "FTC Warns Sneaky Data Brokers Who May Illegally Sell Your Data": *Digital Trends,,* May 8, 2013, http://www.digitaltrends.com/social-media/watch-out-the-ftc-warns-sneaky-data-brokers-who-may-illegally-sell-your-data

along with data on when and what they are willing to spend, to deliver the most relevant messages.[65]

How do consumers feel about the trend to more specific marketing? A December 2013 survey of US digital shoppers, conducted by Harris Interactive, found that the majority of recipients of emails containing personalization drawn from previous shopping behaviors and preferences would be more likely to increase their purchases as a result. In fact, 81 percent of respondents said they were at least somewhat likely to make additional purchases, either online or in store, as a result of targeted emails. Part of this willingness is likely due to the fact that email recipients have already agreed to opt in to receiving messages, making them more accepting of emails with increased relevancy.[66]

> A Wall Street Journal investigation into online privacy has found that the analytical skill of data handlers is transforming the Internet into a place where people are becoming anonymous in name only. The findings offer an early glimpse of a new, personalized Internet where sites have the ability to adjust many things—look, content, prices—based on the kind of person they think you are.[67]

Personalized ads, which deliver sophisticated, individualized mobile messages based on a user's exact

---

[65] Interview with Sheldon Gilbert, CEO Proclivity Media, *Talk Forum NYC*, 10/12/2012, http://www.talkforumnyc.com/2012/10/12/sheldon-gilbert/

[66] Article in *eMarketer*, "Personalization Sees Payoffs" Jan 28, 2014, http://www.emarketer.com/Article/Personalization-Sees-Payoffs-Marketing-Emails/1010563

[67] Steel, Emily, "On the Web's Cutting Edge, Anonymity in Name Only", *Wall Street Journal*, August 4, 2010

location, have also arrived in a big way. In December 2013, Apple activated iBeacon, allowing it to track shoppers (with their permission) in all 254 of its retail locations in the U.S. and send them in-store notifications about upcoming deals and events.

The NFL is following Apple's lead; the same technology (via transmitters) welcomed fans at both Times Square and the 2014 Super Bowl. Once users have downloaded the brand's app and given permission to receive alerts, the NFL can send them location-based messages including directions to a stadium and nearby promotional offers. They can also use algorithms and regression models to figure out behaviors that indicate if a season ticket holder may not renew.[68]

Digital marketing has few boundaries, and encompasses devices such as Smartphones, tablets, laptops, game consoles, televisions, digital billboards, social media, search engines, videos and email. Companies are just scratching the surface on location-based marketing, which uses GPS technology to deliver content based on where a person is located. Are you in a store looking at shoes? Are you buying tickets for a play? Are you eating at your favorite restaurant? Advertisers will send you a message based on where you are and what you are doing at that moment. There are also users who are making their interests known on apps such as Flipboard, Pulse and Foodspotting, which then feed these preferences to merchants and businesses. Data is filtered and customized for each individual, rather

---

[68] Entis, Laura, "The Rise Of Nudge Advertising", *Entrepreneur*.com, Jan. 31. 2014, http://www.entrepreneur.com/article/231200

than grouping like-minded individuals into segments of the population. Now you can be identified individually—talk about a lack of privacy!

If this seems like the future, then the future has arrived. Transmitters are being installed in several hundred stores and public areas in the next few months, including at two dozen Major League Baseball stadiums and a large number of Macy's and American Eagle Outfitters stores.[69]

Popular sites are trying to cash in on your social connections to send advertisements to you. Technology firms like Google, Instagram, Facebook, Pinterest, Twitter and others are increasingly deploying user's data to boost ads.

Pitching a product with a friend's endorsement makes for powerful ads, and the research firm, eMarketer, estimated that the so-called social business advertisements were worth $9.5 billion in U.S. sales in 2013.

This can be a risky business, however. In August, 2013, a judge approved a settlement with Facebook on a class action suit over employing users in ads without their permission. Still, Facebook continues to use 'Likes' and photos in ads targeted to friends. It still is not known if this practice of using endorsements by friends may alienate users and open other companies to privacy lawsuits, but you can be sure a lot of them will try it to gain more advertising dollars.

Ninety-one percent of adult mobile phone owners have their devices within arm's reach 24/7, and location-based

---

[69] Entis, Laura, Ibid

marketing could massively exploit this fact. Furthermore, tools such as Google Wallet are being perfected, which enables people to buy with their credit card right from their Smartphone. The NFC (Near Field Communication) technology in Google Wallet, which allows users to make secure payments, is only set to get better and more popular. Businesses are sure to capitalize on this.[70]

Advertisers have found that videos can convey a more powerful message than text alone and can instantly alter a person's behavior. Were you getting hungry and thinking about a Big Mac? Suppose at lunchtime you got a video message on your phone that Burger King was offering a Whopper for only $1 with a picture of the burger. Would you go there instead?

Do you feel manipulated yet?

YOUR CREDIT SCORE

Where have you shopped lately? Been looking at used cars and second-hand furniture? Have you been to several casinos or a bail-bond service? What you buy and where you shop may affect your credit score. As credit card companies continue to tighten their lending standards on card users, some are using purchased data—gleaned from millions of card transactions processed daily—to weed out those who may or may not be good credit risks. Congress

---

[70] Kaushal, Naveet "Top 5 Digital Marketing Trends of 2014", *ClickZ*, Dec. 3, 2013 *http*://www.clickz.com/clickz/column/2309955/top-5-digital-marketing-trends-of-2014

and federal regulators will be probing the extent to which credit card issuers have used information about where a person shops or what they buy as reasons to lower credit limits or increase interest rates.[71] Thankfully, some congressmen are arguing that what a person spends or where they shop has little bearing on whether they can afford to pay back their credit card so don't abandon those consignment shops yet.

Behavioral modeling, data mining, and psychographic behavior analysis are all ways of searching internal credit card issuer databases for customer spending trends and other patterns. Banks and other financial institutions have been analyzing data and purchases since the beginning of credit cards for several reasons such as:

1. **Marketing**. Issuers use past purchasing patterns as a basis for offering additional products. Someone purchasing camping supplies with a credit card may get offers from wilderness camping cabins, for example.

2. **Law enforcement**. Law enforcement agencies can subpoena records from both the credit card issuer and the merchant to find out the time, date, and place of a credit card purchase—information that may be helpful in determining the last known location of a suspect or a crime victim. The

---

[71] Prater, Connie, "How shopping can affect credit", http://www.creditcards.com/credit-card-news October 14, 2009

Department of Homeland Security also tracks terrorist activity by monitoring certain purchases.

3. **Fraud detection.** Credit card companies monitor cards to detect unusual buying, which might indicate a lost or stolen credit card. Did you spend $300 at Wal-Mart when you have never shopped there before? Did you buy gas in Georgia when you live in Illinois?

4. **Risk management.** Banks know that card users who continually go over their credit limits, use credit card offers of cash or charge large amounts of merchandise on a card may be at greater risk of not paying their bills or filing for bankruptcy.

Thinking of signing up for a credit monitoring service? According to MSN Money, many of these companies tout "free" credit scores, and some even try to pretend they're the official, federally mandated site that offers free credit reports (the real site is AnnualCreditReport.com). Liz Weston of MSN Money says, "way too many readers tell me they had no idea they were signing up for credit monitoring until the charges started appearing on their bills."[72] If a credit-monitoring company gives you free scores, here's the scoop:

---

[72] Weston, Liz ""Is Credit Monitoring a Waste?" *MSNMoney*. MSN Money. Web. 20 Aug. 2012. http://money.msn.com/credit-rating/is-credit-monitoring-a-waste-liz-weston.

- They're probably not the FICO scores that most lenders use, or you're signing up for credit monitoring that isn't free.

- You don't have to spend money to monitor your credit score. You'd typically pay $240 a year for what you can get on your own for free. Use free access to your credit reports at AnnualCreditReport.com. You can get a report once a year from each of the three reporting systems: Experian, Equifax and Transunion. Look at a different one every four months to keep up with your credit score.

- Credit monitoring won't stop bad guys from taking over your credit cards or establishing new accounts in your name. At best, it will give you an early warning that the damage has been done. The "insurance" policies many monitoring companies offer are essentially worthless since most people who are victimized face few, if any, out-of-pocket expenses.[73]

WHAT CAN YOU DO?

The things you can do are pretty much the same as we will be recommending for avoiding identity theft. You should be extremely careful of what you carry in your wallet and don't carry your social security or Medicare card (which has your social security number on it). When disposing of financial documents, shred them. Don't post too much personal

---

[73] Weston, Liz, Ibid

information on social networking sites—especially your date of birth, children's names, first school attended, or your mother's maiden name since those are often used in the challenge questions employed to confirm your identity. Don't answer questions about your financial status or other personal information over the phone, no matter who they say they are. When you receive your bank or credit card statement, review it for errors and charges you did not make.

If you are worried about your account being compromised, you can request a free 90-day fraud alert on your credit reports, which alerts a potential lender to the possibility that your account may have been hacked. Another option is a credit report freeze. This will lock your credit, and if someone applies for credit in your name, the lender won't be able to see your data to approve the application. Credit report freezes may cost you $15 unless you are already a victim of identity theft, in which case you may be able to get one for free.

You can also submit a report about the situation directly to the FTC by completing an Identity Theft Affidavit. First, you will need to file a police report. Then, submit the police report along with the Identity Theft Affidavit to the FTC's Complaint Assistant. After completing the report, you will be given a complaint reference number that you can use to update information at any time.

If your card is stolen or your account compromised, dealing with the problem is usually as simple as reporting it to the creditor. The fraudulent charges are erased and a new credit card with a new account number is issued. You are not held liable for any charges you did not personally make.

A critical thing to remember is that the credit card and other companies start sharing your data after 30 days, so it is up to you to notify them within that time period if you do not want them to share any non-essential data. Here is what you can do.

1. For Capital One, MasterCard, Visa and other credit card companies, you can write or call them and tell them you want to limit sharing of your information. You may not be able to limit all your information based on the agreement you signed.

2. For wireless companies such as Verizon or AT&T, you can notify them via their websites or by calling an 800 number they provide and following their recorded directions. However, if you have a family plan or a multi-line account, you must indicate your choice for each line. If you add a line, you will need to update your privacy choices.

3. Even if you miss notifying a financial or service provider within 30 days, you can still notify them to stop sharing your data. But by then, it may be too late to prevent some of the information from going to other sites. Your providers are not sitting around waiting for you to make up your mind; they want to sell your data as soon as possible.

Identity thieves are sneaky, so you need to be sneaky, too. There are a few simple things you can do to protect your credit card in case it falls into the wrong hands. Sign your credit card with a Sharpie so your signature can't be erased and written over. Some people don't sign it at all but write "See ID" in the signature space. Consultant Sarah Browne of Carmel, California, had all but one credit card stolen from a hotel room. The card that was spared still had the "Please Activate" sticker on it. Though Browne had activated the card, she forgot to remove the sticker. "The thieves must have known that you have to activate a new card from the phone number listed with the credit card company, so they didn't bother with it," she said, and since then, she leaves the activation stickers on all of her cards. Indeed, when a thief struck a second time at a public function, Browne's stickered cards were again left untouched.[74]

IN-STORE AND ONLINE HACKING

It is still unclear how criminals were able to break into many retailers' systems. Target confirmed in December 2013 that criminals had access to its systems by using stolen credentials from a vendor but did not name the vendor. Target tried to minimize the damage by giving its customers free credit reports for a year and a discount of 10 percent over a pre-Christmas weekend, but there are reports that Target has lost many loyal customers. Others swore to only use cash when shopping there in the future.

---

[74] Rogak, Lisa, Ibid

In another hacking incident, Yahoo! said that criminals had gained access to Yahoo! Mail accounts using user names and passwords compromised in a third-party breach.

> In the latest in a spate of online attacks affecting American businesses, White Lodging, which manages hotel franchises for chains like Marriott, Hilton and Starwood Hotels, is investigating a potential security breach involving customers' payment information. A spokesman for the Secret Service could not immediately say whether the agency was investigating the breach of White Lodging data. The Secret Service is conducting separate inquiries into the breaches at Target, Neiman Marcus and Michaels.[75]

Before a transaction can be authorized, credit card data is momentarily decrypted and stored in memory. Thieves have been known to build RAM-scraping malware which scrapes that unencrypted data from memory and steal it. The thefts reignited the push for more secure credit and debit cards, similar to those used in Europe and elsewhere. The result is the EMV chips described in the previous chapter about credit cards. Congress is also calling for tougher consumer protections.

Verizon released their 2013 "Data Breach Investigations Report," which analyzed where the largest threats originate and what cyber-thieves are after when they attack networks. According to the report, a large percentage of these attackers are simply looking for a way to turn a profit, using stolen information on their own or selling it to other parties.

---

[75] Swartz, Walter, "Hotel Company Investigates Data Breach, Card Fraud", *Information Week*, Feb 5, 2014

The majority of the attacks originating in the U.S. are financially motivated. A much smaller percentage of the attacks analyzed in the report were state-affiliated or perpetrated as an act of espionage. The Verizon investigation found that the majority of cyber-espionage attacks originated in East Asia or China.[76]

Verizon said that 75 percent of cyber-attacks were not targeted; companies were hit because criminals saw an opportunity to hack into their systems. The report supports this by saying 78 percent of intrusions required little to no special skills or resources. While these attacks could be deemed simplistic, companies need to protect themselves from data breach or loss, which could have expensive consequences.[77]

WHAT CAN YOU DO?

Is there any way to stop companies from collecting and sharing information about you?

Yes, but it will require a lot of work on your part to stop companies from collecting and sharing your information. Many data brokers offer consumers the chance to "opt out" of being included in their databases or at least from receiving advertising enabled by that company. But to actually opt-out effectively, you need to know about all the different data brokers and where to find their opt-outs. Most

---

[76] Harper, Michael, "Verizon Report States China Is Behind Most US Cyber Attacks", redOrbit.com, April 23, 2013, http://www.redorbit.com/news/technology/1112829171/china-behind-most-cyber-attacks-us-verizon-042313/

[77] Harper, Michael, Ibid

consumers, of course, don't have that information. In their annual privacy report, the FTC suggested that data brokers should create a centralized website that would make it easier for consumers to learn about the existence of these companies and their rights regarding the data they collect.[78]

As with many of the invasions of your privacy, there is little you can do except quit posting all that information about yourself and your family on social media sites. Not only malicious hackers, but "friendly" marketing people are downloading your data and using it in selected ways to manipulate you or your finances. Selling you a product you don't need is not as bad as breaking into your bank account, but both cost you money, and did you really need another dog bed for Fido even if it was a cute tartan?

When you're checking out at a store and a cashier asks you for your ZIP code, don't give it to them. The store isn't just getting that single piece of information. Acxiom and other data companies offer services that allow stores to use your ZIP code and the name on your credit card to pinpoint your home address — without asking you for it directly.[79]

The FTC has released a detailed report calling for Congress to act to give consumers control over the data that companies and data brokers gather and sell. Meanwhile there are online companies out there to help individuals delete these records—but none can guarantee that all data brokers will comply. Regulators and some Congressmen

---

[78] Beckett, Lois, Ibid

[79] Beckett, Lois, Ibid

have been taking a closer look at this industry and are beginning to push the companies to give consumers more information and control over what happens to their data. Companies could voluntarily do this rather than have laws enacted which might be more stringent. The prominent data broker Acxiom recently launched aboutthedata.com, a site that allows you to review some of the information the company has connected to your name—and, potentially, edit and update it as well. For a lasting solution, we need legislation, so contact your state and federal representatives.

Don't expect too much from Congress, however. Marketing companies will probably be excluded from any legislation aimed at financial and medical records. The thinking goes something like this: "What is the worst that could happen? You receive a piece of mail or an advertisement on your Smartphone and all you have to do is get rid of it. It's not like someone stole your identification or your tax records." Yes, congressmen, it's not the end of the world, just another life-hassle for the consumer.

Chapter 5
My Phone Is Selling My Secrets

Members of the House judiciary committee warned the Obama administration and the intelligence agencies that unless they backed a bill to end the bulk domestic phone records collection, they would lose even more counter-terrorism powers under Section 215 when the provision expires in June 2015. That bill, known as the USA Freedom Act, is the chief legislative vehicle to end the mass domestic metadata collection..[80]

Where do government agencies get their information? Your phone company and my phone company are selling our information to the government. While all the phone companies claim that they only do this if there is a court order, your private conversations can be sold for as little as $325 a month if you have AT&T, or $250 a month if you have U.S. Cellular. These are the fees charged to the government for a wiretap for the first month, with continuing fees on a monthly basis. For some reason, Verizon charges the government $775, but don't feel special if you have Verizon; you can still be wiretapped, and the FBI is pushing technology companies like Google and Skype to guarantee real-time communications on their services. If you think this won't happen to you, think again; Sprint had over

---

[80] Ackerman, Spencer, "US intelligence chief: NSA should have been more open about data collection", theguardian.com, Feb18, 2014 http://www.theguardian.com /world/2014/feb/18/us-intelligence-chief-nsa-open-bulk-phone-collection

eight million requests in one year for location data of its wireless customers.[81]

On top of that, law enforcement and the military are using devices called "stingrays" to track cell phones. The government considers these devices sensitive information, and not much is known publicly about how they are used, but it's possible to get a good idea of how they work based on public documents and interviews with technology experts.[82]

The stingray systems involve an antenna, a computer with mapping software and a special device. The device mimics a cell phone tower and gets the phone to connect to it. It can then collect hardware numbers associated with the phone and can ping the cell phone even if the owner isn't making a call. This can be done through walls—something that is useful in finding suspects, as well as victims of crimes or accidents. An antenna pointed at a location can find phones and phone numbers.

Once a signal is found, the stingray measures its strength and can provide a general location on the map. The person manipulating the stingray can then move to another location and again measure the signal strength. By collecting the

---

[81] LaMonica, Paul R., "Government 'spying' on my Verizon phone? Who cares?" *CNN Money*, June 6, 2013: 12:04 PM ET

[82] Valentino-Devries, "'Stingray' Phone Tracker Fuels Constitutional Clash", *Wall Street Journal*, September 22, 2011

signaling information from several locations, the system can triangulate the location of the phone precisely.[83]

Based on many recent articles, our government is also using mass telephonic data mining. It has been reported that the Drug Enforcement Agency secretly uses NSA surveillance data against Americans as part of its "War on Drugs." In other words, the government is outsourcing the automatic collection and storage of millions of Americans' phone records without court approval or oversight—simply so that law enforcement agencies have easy and immediate access to our data in the future. Like the NSA's mass call-tracking program, such extensive and unlimited data gathering, reaching back decades, allows the government to construct incredibly detailed and invasive pictures of our past and present lives.[84]

In July, 2012, the *New York Times* reported that federal, state and local law enforcement officials had requested multiple types of cell phone data, including mappings of suspects' locations, 1.3 million times in the previous year. The FBI also employs highly controversial "tower dumps," where they get the location information on every*one* within a particular radius, potentially violating the privacy of thousands of innocent people with one request.[85]

---

[83] Valentino-Devries, Ibid

[84] Edwards, Eziekel, "Drug Agents Have an NSA-Style Spying Problem", *ACLU Criminal Law Reform Project*

[85] Lightblau, Eric, "Wireless Firms Are Flooded by Requests to Aid Surveillance", *New York Times*, Jul 8, 2012

Now even the Russians are listening in to our conversations. Russia was reported to have monitored all communications of both athletes and spectators at the Sochi Olympics, including those of the U.S. Olympians.

> Athletes and spectators attending the Winter Olympics in Sochi in February, 2014, faced some of the most invasive and systematic spying and surveillance in the history of the Games...newly installed telephone and Internet spying capabilities gave Russia free rein to intercept any telephony or data traffic, and even track the use of sensitive words or phrases mentioned in emails, Web chats and on social media.[86]

Since more people are travelling with Smartphones, there is more to spy on, and the U.S. State Department is warning people traveling abroad to be very careful about what they disclose over their phones. Particularly sensitive is any business or trade secret that could be intercepted and shared with a foreign competitor.

It is also important to note that there are companies that sell mobile phone tracking software to just about anyone. One product advertises that their tracking software "is a powerful mobile monitoring software solution that allows you to track every tiny detail of the target cell phone's activities." This application is easy to use and boasts a wide range of features that make it the best cell phone tracker on the market. In other words, you install this tracking device on your children's phone, your husband's phone or some unsuspecting person's phone and you can track incoming and outgoing calls, see their emails, view their photos and

---

[86] Walker, Shaun, "Russia to monitor 'all communications' at Winter Olympics in Sochi", *The Guardian*, Oct 6 2013

videos, and even track them via GPS. These products are even marketed to companies who want to keep track of their employees as a way to "stop employee dishonesty by monitoring fraudulent behavior." I'd sure like my employer to track my every move, wouldn't you?

E-MARKETING PHONE DATA COLLECTION

Real time bidding is taking place for your phone data. A new e-marketer called Flurry has just become a big-time player with a new way to obtain your data. Flurry started their business by giving away an analytic tool that tells app-makers how people are using their applications. App-makers started embedding it into their products, and now over 400,000 applications use the tool on 1.2 billion phones. Flurry, meanwhile, was able to send most of that data back to themselves, collecting information from approximately seven to ten applications per device.[87]

The problem used to be that advertisers couldn't pinpoint people because unlike desktop computers, which have cookies, phones didn't have tiny data files attached to a browser. Flurry's analytics tool effectively crowd-sources data through applications, encrypting and combining tiny bits of data to create an anonymous ID for each device and grouping them into profiles such as "frequent flyer," "animal lover" or "photographer," for example. These profiles are sold to advertisers, who can then determine

---

[87] Olson, Parmy, "We Know Everything", *Forbes*, November 18, 2013, p.68

which ad to send to which device for maximum profitability.[88]

So far, the U.S. has allowed this type of tracking, but Flurry's policy of encrypting personal information into an anonymous ID has been challenged by some people in the privacy community, particularly in the European Union. The EU already has directives aimed at mobile devices and is tightening the rules. The EU states that end users should be notified of cookies or tracking programs beyond the opt-out option to ensure that when a consumer asks to have his data deleted, the company compiling the data either complies with that request or faces a hefty fine.

USING CALLER ID

Since its introduction, Caller ID has become popular as a way to screen for unwanted calls. It is often used by consumers wishing to avoid telemarketers and those with personal safety concerns.

But, these devices raise privacy issues for both the caller and the person being called. For one thing, Caller ID has become easier to subvert. The ability to send out a false or misleading number to the person called—known as "spoofing"—has serious implications for victims of stalking, harassment and identity theft.

Furthermore, there's the issue of whether you want your telephone number being captured by the place you are

---

[88] Olson, p. 70

calling. If someone does not pick up the phone, the Caller ID device will retain the number—even if it is unlisted—for future viewing. In addition, the time and date of the call are also recorded and displayed. To get around this, you can ask you phone company to install call blocking. If you have blocking and you call someone who subscribes to Caller ID, he will see the message "Private," "P" or "Anonymous" instead of your phone number.

There are many reasons you may want to install call blocking:

1. You do not want your phone number collected for marketing purposes by the businesses you call

2. You are a member of a profession where you do not want your home phone revealed such as a teacher, judge or law enforcement professional

3. You are susceptible to telemarketing pitches

4. You are a victim of harassment or domestic violence.

APPS–ARE THEY SAFE TO DOWNLOAD?

The fun of owning a Smartphone is getting to download a variety of apps including games, music, books and other things of interest. There are thousands of apps covering everything from reminding you to take your medications to identifying constellations in the night sky. Typically you will be in a hurry to download your new app, skip the permissions section and move right on to using the features. Don't do it! You must read the fine print to find out where security issues may arise. Many apps, upon your agreement to the terms and conditions when you download them, help themselves to your personal data, accessing your information, taking pictures with your phone's camera and performing other unwanted activities.

Remember when you make your phone your "best friend" and take it into your confidence, you're also taking in a host of parties that make all of those remarkable mobile services possible including your wireless carrier and phone manufacturer, app developers, mobile advertisers and the maker of your phone's operating system. First, check user reviews to see if anyone has had trouble with the app you want to download.

In the Appthority app reputation report released in February 2013, Appthority reported that 96 percent of iOS aps and 84 percent of Android apps can access at least one of the data risk categories. What's more, apps intended for business use don't behave much better than gaming apps. The data risk categories include the following:

- Accessing the user contacts on a Smartphone (including the contact information that may come from corporate email that syncs to the phone)
- Accessing the user's calendar information
- Collecting or determining the user's location and tracking his movements
- Passing along any or all of this information to ad networks or analytics companies.[89]

---

[89] Appthority Reputation Report, https://www.appthority.com/appreport.pdf

The maker of a popular flashlight app for Android phones agreed to settle charges brought by the FTC that it left consumers in the dark about its data-sharing practice, which transmitted users' location data and device ID numbers to advertising networks and other third parties without the consent or knowledge of the users. The app maker was accused of deceiving consumers into thinking they had the option of not sharing their data when, in fact, they had no control over the data. Regardless of whether users accepted or rejected the terms of the company's license agreement, the flashlight app would transmit location data and device ID information as soon as the consumer launched the application.[90]

WHAT CAN YOU DO?

Most Smartphone owners would rather lose their wallets than their mobile devices. After all, they carry far more sensitive information—private text messages, photos, contacts, addresses, even passwords—in these pocket PCs than they carry in their wallets. Furthermore, mobile phones aren't insured against financial loss the way a credit card is, and a savvy attacker doesn't even need physical access to your device to gather sensitive information including your name, your family and friends, your whereabouts from day to day and passwords to your accounts.

SECURING YOUR PHONE AND DATA FROM THIEVES

Most local phone companies offer a service called Privacy Manager. It works with Caller ID to identify incoming calls

---

[90] Vijayan, Jaikumar, "Flashlight app vendor settles with FTC over privacy violations", *ComputerWorld*, Dec. 6, 2013, http://computerworldcom/s/article/9244612

that have no telephone numbers. Calls identified as "anonymous," unavailable," out of area" or "private" must identify themselves in order to complete the call. When your phone rings, you can choose to accept or reject the call, send it to voicemail or send a special message to telemarketers instructing them to put you on their "do not call" list.

Having your Smartphone stolen is bad enough—you're out the money that the phone originally cost and you have to buy a new one—but the idea that the thief now has access to your personal data stored on the phone is even worse. Luckily, there are steps you can take before your phone is lost or stolen, that can protect your data. The most important is setting a strong password that will force someone to enter it when they want to access your phone. If the thief doesn't know your password, he can't access your data.

Another way to make sure a thief can't get your data is to set your Smartphone to automatically delete all its data when an incorrect password is entered a certain number of times. If you're not good at remembering your password, you may want to be careful, but this is one of the best ways to protect your phone. This will be an option on your phone when you set up a password.[91]

Some applications are moving to security measures like fingerprints instead of passwords. The latest iPhone 5S

---

[91] Costello, Sam, "How to Protect Data on Lost or Stolen iPhone", About.Com, http://ipod.about.com/od/iphonetroubleshooting/tp/Protect-Data-On-Lost-Or-Stolen-Iphone.htm

boasts a new feature aimed at increasing privacy protection: a fingerprint scanner that is embedded into the home button. This lets phone owners log in to their Smartphone without using a number password. For added security, user fingerprint data will not be accessible through a cloud server but rather on the "Secure Enclave" in a chip on the iPhone.

And for those willing to spend over $500 for a phone, Boeing is developing a Smartphone that has built-in disk encryption that protects stored data by converting it to garbled code. Try to take it apart and it self-destructs. Another maker, SGP Technologies, has a phone called "Blackphone" that allows users to block everyday applications like Facebook from tapping into their locations, contacts and other data.[92]

To guard against theft of your phone or data, follow these tips:

- Disable your location tracking except when you need it for driving directions or finding a nearby store. If your phone's operating system lets you turn it off for individual apps, use that feature for greater control.

- Before you sell or recycle your phone, delete all data, remove your memory card from your old phone and restore its factory settings.

- Don't click on pop-up links that come in unsolicited or unfamiliar links within a text message. Links in

---

[92] Lev, Ram, Michal, "The Most Secure Phones on Earth", *Fortune*, Apr 7, 2014, p. 36

text spam can lead to websites that download malicious software of the sort that e-mail scammers have used for years. You can go to your wireless carrier's website and ask to have texts sent over the Internet blocked, or you can install an app that can block them.

- Don't engage in financial transactions at hotspots in hotels, airports, retail stores or coffee houses, because they may have insecure Wi-Fi. Before using any app to do business at a hotspot, check its privacy policy to see whether it secures wireless transmission of such data. Otherwise that account number or password you disclosed could be intercepted.

- If you do download apps, choose them from a reputable brand and make sure their user reviews include no credible complaints about security or privacy concerns. If an app uses sensitive personal information, make sure the app can't be used without entering a password.

- Back up important data. Your phone company may provide a free backup service. If not, find a highly-recommended company to do this for you.

- Finally, don't use your phone to store sensitive data such as PINs or passwords for your accounts or your social security number.

Free apps have more security issues than paid apps, but even with the paid apps, half have tracking devices built in. The popular free apps are more likely to collect data about the user and sell it to outside parties and it will come as no surprise that gaming and entertainment apps lead the way in sharing data.[93]

Percent of Mobile Phone Users Who:

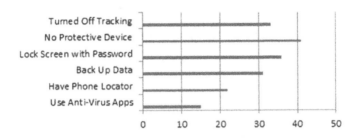

Poll taken by Consumer Reports, 2013

Even though the majority of Americans say they are very concerned about their personal data when they buy a mobile phone, very few are motivated enough to change their habits or buy security software.[94]

There are many security apps that have been installed by thousands of Smartphone users to try to protect their personal information from being downloaded to some data broker or hacker. Some are free and some have a yearly fee, usually around $20-$30. Listed are some popular ones that help secure data and pictures from thieves—but not necessarily from government agencies. And if your phone is

---

[93] Appthority Ibid

[94] Consumer Reports, "How to protect yourself from wireless threats"; June 2013, http://www.consumerreports.org/content/dam/cro/news_articles/Electronics/consumer_reports

stolen, you'll want to make sure to secure all aspects of your digital life, not just your phone. Change your other online passwords, including email, to stop the thief from sending mail from your phone.

Lookout (Available for Android or iPhone)

The mobile security software offers real-time protection, GPS locating features and the ability to lock and wipe your phone remotely. One of the standout features of this security application is the ability to back up your data to a secure cloud-based account and then restore it again when you feel it is safe to do so.

Disconnect (Available for iPhone)

Disconnect is a mobile app for children that will keep trackers and third parties from gathering information from kids' phones.

HiddenEye (Available for Android; Free)

HiddenEye uses your Smartphone's camera in self-defense: This app photographs any person who tries to unlock your phone.

Find My iPhone (Available for iPhone)

If you misplace your iPhone, the Find My iPhone app will let you use another iOS device to find it and protect your data. Locates the missing device on a map, plays a sound, displays a message, remotely locks the device and/or erases all the data on it.

SeekDroid (Available for Android; Free)

SeekDroid (similar to Find My iPhone) allows the user to locate a lost or stolen Android device. It features device location on a map, remote audible alarm, remote wiping of the device, remote tracking and GPS.

Avast Free Mobile Security (Available for Android; Free)

Famous from the PC space, Avast also has an antivirus and anti-theft Android security application. It includes scanning of installed apps and memory card content on demand. It also features a privacy report, which scans and displays access rights and intents of installed apps, as well as anti-theft components that give the user remote control via SMS or Web to lock, locate, or wipe the device of data.

AVG Mobilation Antivirus (Available for: Android; Free)

AVG's version of antivirus for Smartphones detects harmful apps and text messages. Features include scanning of apps, settings, files and media in real time; location of lost or stolen phone via Google Maps; lock and wipe device to protect privacy.

ESET Mobile Security & Antivirus (Free)

Provides real-time scanning of apps to detect malware and dubious apps trying to send texts or make premium rate calls. The free version also includes a suite of anti-theft tools. You can remotely locate and lock your smartphone or tablet, and you can prevent anyone from uninstalling apps by using password protection.

Some of these security applications are platform-specific and may not be relevant to all Smartphone users, but the ever-changing nature of threats to mobile devices is such that you should keep informed about security measures and products. Keep in mind that hackers, malicious users and thieves are usually opportunists and would rather target those who have offered them an easy way to achieve their goals than spend time working around obstacles. Follow the advice we have offered to make sure you and your phone aren't easy targets and you'll stay one step ahead of the bad guys.

Chapter 6

Help! My Identity Has Been Hacked

The University of Delaware joined the long line of recent data breach victims with a compromised university system yielding personal information on 72,000 past and present employees.[95]

IDENTITY THEFT

You may have locked up your house but what about the most vulnerable place to lose your money: your computer or the computer of someone you have trusted to guard your sensitive data. An identity thief will never have to meet you personally or set foot in your home if he can access your computer to find your tax returns, birth date and account numbers to steal your money.

All too frequently we read about some system being hacked and personal data stolen. We have given our data to multiple financial and social institutions, trusting that they will guard that data with firewalls, encryption, security procedures and vetted employees. Often that trust is misplaced; companies are operating with antiquated security or poor procedures for checking the backgrounds of

---

[95] Dobo, Nichole, "Hackers Steal Identity Info of 72,000 at U of Delaware", *The (Wilmington, Del.) News Journal*, July 31, 2013

employees who have access to sensitive data. Many don't upgrade until a problem happens and they are forced to do something about it. Online stores are a big target for hackers; brands like Polo, BJ's Wholesale, Target, DSW Shoes, T.J. Maxx, and iTunes have all made the news recently for losing their customer data.

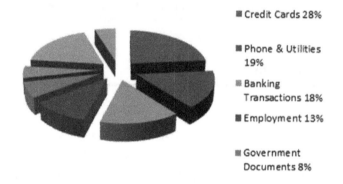

- Credit Cards 28%
- Phone & Utilities 19%
- Banking Transactions 18%
- Employment 13%
- Government Documents 8%

How Your Identity is Stolen

The average person doesn't want to ask their bank, doctor or employer what safeguards they have for protecting sensitive data. Even when asked, unless the person is an IT person working in the security division, most don't really know. Consequently, we have to depend on the company or person to whom we are entrusting our data that it is secure.

> Hackers stole credit card and tax information from 3.6 million people in South Carolina. They obtained the data by hacking into the state's Department of Revenue—a hole that the DOR says it has now patched up—but it took ten days to close the hacker's access, during which 387,000 credit and debit card numbers, along with social security numbers, were exposed.[96]

[96] Pardue, Doug, "Revenue Department Hacking Leaves Millions of S.C. Residents at Risk for Life", (Charleston, SC) Post and Courier, Aug 21, 2013

"A New Card Is on the Way." Along with thousands of other people, this is the message I received recently from my credit card company. "We are sending you a new credit card with a new number. It will arrive in the next several days. Your current card was identified as at risk from Target's data security breach. This occurred because you used it at a Target store between November 27th and December 15th. Our experienced Fraud Detection team will continue to monitor your account to help identify any unusual activity. If we detect it, we will notify you."[97] Great, but I didn't really want another credit card number; I wanted my data to be protected!

> The data breach at Target was significantly broader than originally reported: The company said that 70 million customers had information such as their name, address, phone number and e-mail address hacked in the breach, and as many as 40 million customers may have also had credit or debit card information stolen.[98]

The stories we read in the newspaper are usually the huge thefts of data, but most of the data bought and sold through computer hacking, including stolen credit card numbers, passwords, security questions and answers, bank account numbers, email addresses and social security numbers, is stolen from personal computers that are either not protected or protected with an password that is easy for hackers to guess.

---

[97] Information from Chase Credit Card Fraud Department

[98] Isadore, Chris, CNNMoney, "Target: Hacking hit up to 110 million customers", January 11, 2014

Criminal organizations around the world are becoming very involved in computer hacking, and most of that data will end up on a network of illegal trading sites where criminals can openly buy and sell personal data for profit. One network named Shadowcrew is believed to have had thousands of members who made millions of dollars in less than two years trading 1.5 stolen credit cards.[99] This network has now been shut down, but others have sprung up to take its place. Some stolen credit card sites even have a rating system where members can post feedback on the quality of the stolen credit cards and some will take orders for specific types of stolen credit cards. This may seem unbelievable, but hacking accounts for the largest amount of compromised personal records and the number of accounts hacked grows larger every year. In the case of the recent Target hacking, over 110 million people were compromised.

Between credit cards or debit cards, it is the debit card holders who are most at risk since debit cards are tied directly to your bank account. If money is fraudulently withdrawn from your account, it can cause legitimate transactions to fail. You may have a monthly debit set up for a mortgage for example, and if your account has been compromised, your mortgage will not be paid on time. According to David Uffington, there are some places you should think twice about using your debit card such as a gas pump (you should go into the station to do your transaction); online, because too many sites aren't secure

---

[99] Zetter, Kim, "9 Years After Shadowcrew, Feds Get Their Hands on Fugitive", *Wired*, July 1, 2013, http://www.wired.com/threatleven/2013/07/bulgarian-shadowcrew-arrest/

enough; and any ATM that is not out in public because an out-of-the-way location is easier to tamper with.[100]

One of the more common hacking concepts is to wait for the victims to come to the hacker. This is accomplished by identifying a website frequently visited by employees of a targeted corporation. Then the legitimate site is hacked and an exploit or trojan planted on some of the pages. When employees visit the infected pages, their computers are compromised, allowing hackers access to the organization's internal resources and private information.

You may think that your computer is safe but here are some of the ways a professional hacker can launch an attack:

- Hiding malicious code in images on websites

- Sending bogus emails that the unwary user clicks on

- Exploiting browser vulnerabilities that have not been properly patched

- Attacking a computer that doesn't have a firewall installed

- Exploiting poorly installed home networks

- Installing keystroke loggers

- Exploiting weak passwords.

---

[100] Uffington David, "Debit Card Safety", *Tidbits of Baldwin County, King Features Synd., Inc,* Feb. 12, 2014

> The FBI and other U.S. agencies said ... they were investigating a website that posted financial and personal information about first lady Michelle Obama, Vice President Joe Biden, and other government figures as well as celebrities including singers Beyoncé and Jay-Z. The hacker, who is being hunted by law enforcement, reportedly forwarded the sensitive information on to a website.[101]

According to the FBI, in the case of the celebrity hacking, some of the information was fraudulently obtained via Equifax, a commonly used website for consumer credit reports. It was unclear how much of the data was accurate, but the site listed social security numbers, telephone numbers, addresses and credit reports purportedly belonging to 18 prominent Americans. Some of the telephone numbers are known to be inaccurate. Other well-known people listed on the page included FBI Director Robert Mueller, Attorney-General Eric Holder, former Secretary of State Hillary Clinton, Los Angeles Police Chief Charlie Beck, actors Ashton Kutcher and Arnold Schwarzenegger and property mogul Donald Trump.[102]

Asked about the posting, Equifax company spokesman Timothy Klein said, "The fraudsters would have had to have a lot of information...this is pretty detailed stuff. Those responsible for the breach would have had to know about mortgages, car loans, or other credit accounts to get the reports." He added, "[B]ut we are actually taking the

---

[101] Dillon, Nancy & Tracy, Thomas, "Hacker Takes Info", *New York Daily News*, March 11, 2013

[102] Dillon, Nancy & Tracy, Thomas, Ibid

necessary steps to further improve and tighten the credentialing process".[103]

> Ben Bernacke, the Federal Reserve Board Chairman, was one of the victims of a scam artist known as "Big Head" who stole more than $2 million from consumers and at least ten financial institutions.[104]

When it comes to data security, end users are often the weakest link. The new Cloud applications are becoming primary targets for attacks because they are accessible from anywhere in the world and many of the hackers are from developing economies with a low-paid but highly skilled workforce that can be used for illegal activities. There have been several articles written about the weaknesses in some high profile Internet and Cloud applications including LinkedIn, Yahoo!, eHarmony, Zappos and Sony—all of which have been hacked. These applications are developing, or have developed, more complex hashing algorithms and are using salts for password hashing.

Salts are random pieces of data that are used as an additional input to a one-way function that hashes a password. The primary purpose of a salt is to defend against hacker attacks. Salts also make dictionary attacks and brute force attacks, used for cracking large numbers of passwords, much slower. Without salts, an attacker who is cracking many passwords at the same time only needs to hash each

---

[103] Oliveira, Pedro Jr., "U.S. probes hack of personal data on Michelle Obama, Beyoncé, others" *Reuters, Washington,* Mar 12, 2013 5:12pm EDT

[104] Dillon, Nancy & Tracy, Thomas, Ibid

password guess once and compare it to all the hashes. However, with salts each password will likely have a different salt, so each guess would have to be hashed separately for each salt. This is much slower and makes it more expensive to try to hack such systems.

A lot of Cloud services have technical users who should have secure passwords, but the majority of the Cloud services allow simple passwords with any characters; consequently most of those passwords tend to be very short. This means hackers can easily guess user passwords using simple online techniques that do not compromise the cloud applications. Research data has shown that some of the services require only a one-character password, and only a few cloud services use passwords with six or more characters containing upper and lower case letters and numbers along with special characters.[105]

Services dealing with billing and payments should be using very strict passwords, but the argument is that people can't remember long, complicated passwords and that when people are forced to change their passwords periodically, people want a simple password that they can easily guess. Some applications are moving to other security measures, like fingerprints instead of passwords, but there are already stories about hackers being able to access this type of security.

---

[105] Londis, Dino, "10 Top Password Managers", *Computerworld,* Apr 30, 2013, http://www.informationweek.com/security/risk-management/10-top-password-managers

A recent search by a large internet company revealed that countless printers, servers and system control devices use "admin" as their user name and "1234" as their password. Many more connected systems require no credentials at all—all you need is a Web browser to connect to them.

In an article in *Money*, the magazine stated that "the number one way hackers get into protected systems isn't through a fancy technical exploit. It's by guessing the password. That's not too hard when the most common password used on business systems is "Password1."[106]

Having complicated passwords may become easier in the future. Motorola is developing an edible password. That's right; you swallow a pill each day that contains a tiny chip. The chip uses the acid in your stomach to power it on. Once activated, it emits a specific 18-bit, EKG-like signal that can be detected by your phone or computer, essentially turning your body into a password.[107]

Most people know there is no government official in Ghana who is going to split millions of dollars with them if they send him information and a "token" amount of money, but here are some other ways hackers get you to reveal information online:

- "Hi, this is Joe from IT and your computer has been infected with the xyz virus." Hackers often take advantage of the latest malware scare and tell the

---

[106] Pagliery, Jose, "How not to get hacked", *CNN Money*, Dec. 5, 2013, http://money.cnn.com/gallery/technology/2013/12/05/password-hack/

[107] Time Staff, "The 25 Best Inventions of the Year", *Time*, Nov. 13, 2013, pg. 74

employee they will fix their computer but they need their password. The employee figures it is someone he can trust and gives out his password, which is then used to access the computer and steal whatever company information they can get.

- Or the email purporting to be from HR that says "We need to verify your social security number in order to deposit your paycheck in your bank account". And by the way, they may ask you to verify your bank account number too!

- Phishing emails that prompt recipients to open a fake message. This may be from one of your relatives or friends who have already had their email account hacked. Once the recipient opens the email, a trojan is placed on their system that steals data, particularly banking information.

- "You have not paid for the item you ordered on eBay." People who bid on eBay or other bidding sites often fall for this one just to see which of their bids was accepted.

- "Take this survey and get a free gift card." All you will get is your personal information stolen. Retailers are not giving free gift cards for taking surveys.

- "Have you seen that blog about you?" This ploy is used on social media sites like Twitter and Facebook, which then sends the curious person to a fake login screen to reveal his logon information.

- "Your bank account has been closed." This is used to get you to panic and give out bank account information, again on a fake login screen.

- "Donate to Haitian victims." These sites spring up every time there is a disaster, be it Hurricane Sandy or flooding in Iowa. The goal is to get well-meaning people to donate to the relief funds using their credit cards. As you can imagine, the credit card information is then sold or used to make fraudulent purchases.

- "The IRS needs your information to send you a refund." The IRS warns taxpayers that they never initiate contact by email to request personal information or inform you that you are being electronically audited or getting a refund. If you receive such an email, report it to phishing@irs.gov.

WHAT CAN YOU DO?

You can take steps to minimize privacy issues and identity theft risks associated with your digital footprint, but it is important to realize that it is virtually impossible to entirely erase it. Instead, focus on management techniques to ensure your footprint is as small as possible and only reflects the things you want to share:

1. Carefully review privacy settings on all your social media accounts and choose settings that ensure the maximum protection for your information.

2. Open your Web browser and search for your own name. Take steps to remove your information from mailing lists and Web lists.

3. Regularly clear cookies and history from your browser, especially if you've used a public PC (such as in a hotel business center) for personal business. You can do this by clicking on **Tools** and then **Internet Options**. Next click on the **General tab**. Under Browsing History, click **Delete**. Choose **Delete Files** and click **Yes**. Next Choose **Delete Cookies** and click **Yes**. Close and click **OK**. Restart your browser.

4. When working online, always read a website's privacy statement before entering any personal information on the site.

5. When shopping online, only deal with reputable websites that have demonstrated security measures in place.

6. Avoid conducting personal online business over unsecured wireless networks such as in airports or at a coffee house.

Identify theft can occur even if you have been very diligent about guarding your data. If the worst happens, three basic steps need to be taken:[108]

---

[108] Federal Trade Commission "When Bad Things Happen To Your Good Name", *FTD*, Sept. 2002

1. Contact the fraud department of the three major credit bureaus and tell them you are a victim of identity theft.

2. File a police report and provide as much documentation as you can with an ID Theft Affidavit. If local authorities tell you they can't take the report, stress the importance of a police report in case there is a dispute with one of your financial companies.

3. Cancel all credit cards, including store cards, and tell them why you are cancelling so they can also put a fraud alert on your cards.

You can also go to the website www.irs.gov/uac/Identity-Protection for steps to help you protect against tax-related identity theft. Here are some of their suggestions, which are similar to ones documented from other sources:

*   Don't carry your social security card or any document(s) with your social security number (SSN) on it.

*   Don't give a business your SSN just because they ask. Give it only when required.

*   Protect your financial information.

*   Secure personal information in your home.

*   Protect your personal computers by using firewalls, anti-spam/virus software, update security patches, and change passwords for Internet accounts.

- Don't give personal information over the phone, through the mail or on the Internet unless you have initiated the contact or you are sure you know who you are dealing with.[109]

Identity theft is a serious infringement not only on a person's finances, but also potentially on his time. People who have had their identities stolen can spend months, and sometimes years, cleaning up the mess thieves have made of their good name and credit record. Victims have been refused loans, denied benefits, lost a job opportunity and in extreme cases even been wrongly arrested because of something they had no control over.

Be constantly on guard and try to limit the amount of personal information you share with others, both on the Internet and through your day-to-day activities.

THIRD-PARTY HACKING

Software installed by vendors is a tempting target for hackers who infiltrate seemingly innocuous devices—video-conference equipment, thermostats, vending machines, printers and other decides that are remotely monitored. Hackers in the recent Target payment card breach apparently gained access to the retailer's records through its heating and cooling system.[110]

---

[109] www.irs.gov/uac/Identity-Protection

[110] Perlroth, Nicole, "Hackers Lurking in Vents and Soda Machines", NY Times, Apr 8, 2014, p. A1

Hackers have been known to go so far as to install malware on soda machines, and in one instance the online menu of a restaurant that was popular with employees of an oil company. A survey of more than 3,500 global I.T. and cyber-security practitioners conducted by the Ponemon Institute, found that 23 percent of breaches were attributable to third-party negligence.[111] One reason is that only five percent of retail I.T. spending goes to security measures, while the majority is spent on customer marketing and data analytics. In comparison, banks spend on average 12 percent of their information budget on security.[112]

SHODAN

Unlike Google, which searches for websites, Shodan, invented by John Matherly, is the world's first computer search engine that lets you search the Internet for computers and find devices based on city, country, latitude/longitude, hostname, operating system and IP. Shodan runs 24/7 and collects information on about 500 million connected devices and services each month.

Experts say that many of the devices that Shodan finds shouldn't be online at all. Companies will often buy systems that can enable them to control devices such as a heating system with a computer. Rather than connect them directly to a computer, some IT departments just plug them into a

---

[111] Ponemon, Institute, quoted in the *New York Times,* http://www.ponemon.org/news-2/48

[112] Perlroth, Nichole, Ibid

Web server, inadvertently sharing them with the rest of the world.

> Shodan searchers have found control systems for a water park, a gas station, a hotel wine cooler and a crematorium. Cyber-security researchers have even located command and control systems for nuclear power plants and a particle accelerating cyclotron. It's astonishing what can be found with a simple search on Shodan. Countless traffic lights, security cameras, home automation devices and heating systems are connected to the Internet and easy to spot.[113]

The good news is that Shodan limits searches to just ten results without an account and 50 with an account. If you want to see everything Shodan has to offer, Matherly requires more information about what you're hoping to achieve—and a fee. There are about a dozen users, all of them cyber-security firms that pay big bucks to access Shodan's entire database of 1.5 billion connected devices. Security professionals, academic researchers and law enforcement agencies are the primary users of Shodan, and by finding systems that are unsecured and vulnerable, these professionals can warn users of the potential for harm.[114]

The bad news is that hackers have also been able to find webcams and other devices with low security using Shodan. Dan Tentler, a security researcher, has documented millions of exposed webcams in operating rooms, child care centers,

---

[113] Goldman, David "A New Program for Hackers to (Mis) Use", *CNN Money*, April 8, 2013

[114] Goldman, David, Ibid

people's homes and even security offices and traffic lights. Tentler says, "It's like crack for voyeurs."[115]

Many people think that John Matherly and Shodan should be praised for calling attention to the millions of unprotected webcams and other products that companies make with little or no security. Everything that connects to the Internet should be password-protected, but many are not or have a default password like "admin." Just one more thing to consider when buying a home security system or hooking up your heating or cooling system to the Internet.

> Most people have heard of the Houston resident who got the scare of his life when he walked into his two-year-old's room and heard a voice coming over the baby monitor saying "Wake up, you little slut." Someone had taken control of the camera and the audio. It was later found that a flaw in the product allowed hackers to take control of the monitor by using the user name "admin."[116]

WHAT CAN YOU DO?

Many Internet companies are trying to make themselves safer from cyber-attacks by adding two-step authentication. For example, users of the professional social-networking site LinkedIn, along with Google, Apple and Facebook, now have the option to add two-step verification to their accounts. This is designed to add another layer to the sign-in process when logging in from a new or unknown device.

---

[115] Goldman, David, Ibid

[116] Ngak, Chenda Ngak, "Baby monitor hacked, spies on Texas child", *CBS News*, August 13, 2013 http://www.cbsnews.com/news/baby-monitor-hacked-spies-on-texas-child/

With the feature enabled, users will be prompted to type a numeric code sent to their phone via SMS. LinkedIn has said that most Internet accounts that have become compromised are illegitimately accessed from a new computer or device.[117]

Encryption dramatically increases email security, which is why Google is now not only encrypting all mail as it travels across the net between user's devices and Gmail servers but also as it moves between machines within its data centers.[118]

Twitter has also introduced two-factor authentication following a series of recent hacks targeting high-profile businesses on the blogging site. Last year, users were advised to change their passwords after it was reported that millions of "unsalted" hashed passwords had turned up on a Russian hacker website.

But while a two-factor login and increased encryption adds an extra layer of security, it is not a panacea, some security experts have said. With an email phishing attack, for instance, a hacker could fake a login page to ask for the code the user just received. There seems to be no end to the tricks a hacker can use to get your data so you have to be on the alert every time you put your personal data where others can see it.

---

[117] Silveira,Vincente, "Protecting your LinkedIn Account with Two-Step Verification", *LinkedIn blog*; http://blog.linkedin.com/2013/05/31/protecting-your-linkedin-account-with-two-step-verification/

[118] McCracken, Harry, "Email providers get serious about security", Time, Apr 7, 2014 p. 22

Some other easy steps you can personally take to make it harder for hackers to find your data are:

- Make sure all computers you use, both at home and at the office, have the latest firewalls and anti-virus software installed.

- Don't open suspicious emails—don't just look at the name of the person who sent them but also the subject line, your friend's email may have been hacked.

- Be careful about the types of websites you click on and/or download from.

- Educate everyone who uses your computer about security risks.

- Keep up-to-date with patches, particularly for your browser.

IDENTITY THEFT

In one day you might write a check at a grocery store, use your credit card for lunch at a restaurant, file your tax return online, charge tickets to a play and look up your 401K returns at your financial institution. You may not give these everyday activities a second thought, but an identity thief may be lurking at any of these sites to steal your information.

According to AARP, the elderly are the most vulnerable segment of the population subject to identity theft; last year,

Americans 50+ accounted for about half of the losses from these schemes. These range from being told they missed a loan payment to bogus threats about utilities being shut off to fake court summons. In these cases scammers scared seniors into revealing their personal information and used the stolen data for everything from bogus check writing scams to credit card fraud.[119]

Some examples of the many ways criminals use stolen identity information are to:

- Steal money from the victim's existing accounts
- Obtain credit fraudulently from banks and retailers
- Apply for loans
- Establish accounts with utility companies
- Rent an apartment
- File for bankruptcy
- Obtain a new credit card
- Get a wireless phone in your name
- Obtain a job
- Receive medical care
- Counterfeit checks
- Achieve other financial gain using the victim's name

The cyber dictionary NetLingo defines a digital footprint as "the trail you leave in cyberspace and on any form of digital communication." [120] In other words, everything you do in cyberspace—emails, text messages, Web browsing, logging on or off a network, playing video games—leaves a trail.

---

[119] Kirchheimer, Sid, "Protect Your Wallet", AARP Bulletin, Oct, 2013, p. 14

[120] www.netlingo.com

Some of the information that makes up that trail are things you voluntarily share, such as anything on your social network profile, but other aspects occur invisibly without your express consent or knowledge.

Identity thieves and other cyber crooks can use your digital footprint to collect data and misuse your personal identifying information. It pays to not only be aware of your digital footprint, but to also take steps to manage it. You do not want an unknown person to access your Facebook account to find out your children's names or other sensitive data.

> Security is a race between the good guys and the bad guys. After being a professional hacker for a number of years, breaking into computer networks and breaking into physical buildings to get access to computer networks and data, I learned that the things I was able to do most successfully often had very little to do with technology. I could spend a week, a month or three months pounding on an Internet-connected network for some agency trying to sneak past their firewall, or in a matter of two days I could actually be inside the building through social engineering. Maybe by creating a fake badge that looked like an employee badge, pretending to be a telephone repairman, or even by entering through the smokers' entrance. There's a whole pile of stuff that doesn't involve technology.[121]

Most of us have only a rudimentary understanding of how to follow our own digital footprints (think backtracking through your browser history to find that site you accessed the last week). Cyber crooks, however, know how to track your trail straight to usable information, and with the

---

[121] Long, Johnny, *IRMUK* Data Management Conference Speech, London, 2011

widespread use of mobile devices such as Smartphones and tablets, the average person's digital footprint has grown even larger. Criminals will often take weeks and months getting to know a company before even coming in the door. Posing as a client or service technician is one of many possibilities. Knowing the right thing to say, who to ask for and having confidence are often all it takes for an unauthorized person to gain access, and once they have access there is no end to the amount of personal data they can steal about the people who work at that company.

Scammers don't need to be master hackers to break into your bank account. A pen and paper can be enough—especially if the paper comes from a lost or stolen checkbook. Cybercrimes may rule the headlines, but old school scams are making a comeback—and some of them never really went away. Check fraud, for example, is one of the oldest forms of payment fraud and one of the most persistent. About 87 percent of financial professionals said their companies experienced check fraud, according to the 2013 Payments Fraud and Control survey.[122]

Check fraud continues to be a problem for a number of reasons. Billions of checks are processed every year, making it challenging to do a review of each check to prevent fraud. Plus, criminals now have easy access to basic desktop publishing tools for printing fake checks.

---

[122] Report of Survey Results, Underwritten by J. P. Morgan https://www.jpmorgan.com/cm/BlobServer/2013_AFP_Payments_Fraud_Survey.pdf

Another kind of identity theft is called synthetic identify theft. Instead of stealing an actual person's identity, a thief creates a fictional identity by taking pieces of information from a number of people and using one person's social security number creates a fictional identity associated with that number. This type of identity theft is often harder to detect than true identity theft because accounts and other credit that is falsely obtained this way typically do not show up on the credit report of the victim whose social security number has been stolen.

Identify theft has become so prevalent that Hollywood recently made a successful comedy about a man who chases a woman who has been living it up using his identity. While the movie is very entertaining, the real thing is anything but a comedy. It can be both infuriating and disturbing to think someone else is posing as you.

Chapter 7

Give to a Worthy Cause—Not to Scammers

He claimed to be a retired Naval commander and raised more than $100 million from generous Americans for his charity in Tampa. He told his lawyer he got funding for a U.S. Navy Veterans Association from a "black box" CIA budget and said in court filings that he was working under "non-official cover" for the agency. But in the end, a jury here decided that Bobby Thompson, 66, was less James Bond and more run-of-the-mill con man. ... They convicted him on 23 counts of fraud, money laundering and theft in a charity scam.[123]

CHARITIES

It was December. I was feeling the holiday spirit and decided to give money to a school for poor American Indian kids in Oklahoma. They thanked me profusely by mail and even sent me a "genuine" spirit necklace made out of plastic. But then, just when I was feeling good about myself, I decided to look up the charity on an online charity evaluator—and you guessed it—it was one of the worst in America. The kids got about 12 percent of the funds; the rest went to the fundraising organization.   And, of course, I keep getting cards, address labels, calendars and more pleas for donations, from that school and many other 'schools'.

---

[123] Charity Watch "Hall of Shame", http://www.charitywatch.org/articles/CharityWatchHallofShame.html

I'm sure we all have made donations to dubious organizations that sounded like they were doing good work, whether it was for tornado victims, cancer patients or a veteran's organization. How many of us have had our arms twisted to donate to one cause or another by our friends, pledge drives at work or even the schools our kids attend?

A ballpark figure for a reputable charity is about 10 percent administrative cost, about 10 percent cost for personnel, and about 25 percent cost for advertising. The rest should go to the purpose of the charity whether it is disaster relief, fighting a disease, ongoing charitable relief for the poor or saving wildlife.

The 50 worst charities in America devote less than four percent of the donations they collect to direct cash aid. Some charities give even less. Over a decade, one diabetes charity raised nearly $14 million and gave about $10,000 to patients. Even as they plead for money, the organizers and fund raisers pay themselves exorbitant salaries and consulting fees or arrange fundraising contracts with friends. One cancer charity paid a company owned by the president's son nearly $18 million over eight years to solicit funds.[124]

Your decision to make a donation is generous, but you need to be vigilant if you plan to make that donation online. Scammers are looking to steal not just your money, but also your personal information. Bogus groups are hard to tell apart from legitimate non-profits, and there are now almost

---

[124] Hundley, Chris & Taggert, Kendall, "America's Worst Charities", *Tampa Bay Times*, June 6, 2013

two million non-profits in the United States[125]—all of them looking for money.

The most recent data shows that in 2012, individual Americans donated $45 billion to charity.[126] But while giving has increased, so has the number of fraudulent charities, reports the U.S. Department of Justice. The tactics range from the high-tech to low-tech. Phishing, for example, is a real hazard; users simply click on an email link that leads to a bogus Website that appears legit but isn't. Instead, the users' credit card information and passwords are stolen. Another tactic is to use a celebrity as the "face" of the charity because most people believe a celebrity wouldn't lend his face and name to a bogus scheme.[127]

The purpose of any charity is to provide some public benefit to a community or to people's lives. To determine if a charity is getting good results, you can begin by learning about a charity's programs, accomplishments, goals and challenges. You can do this by reviewing its website where they should list how their programs lead to results. Beware of "sound alike" organizations that have names similar to responsible, reputable charities. Don't be swayed merely by a benevolent-sounding name. Scammers will use guilt, compassion, poverty and hardship as manipulation tactics.

---

125   Guidestar   blog,   http://www.guidestar.org/rxg/give-to-charity/donor-resources/review-a-charity.aspx

126 Giving USA 2012: "The Annual Report on Philanthropy for the Year"

127 Ellin, Abby, "Charity Fraud, Is That Celeb Legit?", ABC News, June 12, 2011, http://abcnews.go.com/Business/protect-charity-fraud/story?id=16468471

And never, ever give out credit card, bank account or other personal information over the phone.

Some experts advise against giving small amounts of money because they say it will only cause you to end up on many mailing lists. Donations under $25 barely cover the costs of soliciting the gift. To recoup those costs, many charities will simply sell the donor's name to another charity doing similar work. These same experts say that giving one larger gift instead of many small ones will protect you because charities are in competition with each other for your donation. The revenue generated by selling your information simply doesn't outweigh the risk of losing you to another charity. However, there are many organizations who welcome donations of $25. Many of them are local charities, such as food banks and homeless shelters that have no intention of selling your data.

Unless you've signed up to receive a charity's electronic communications, be skeptical of email solicitations. Although you may receive an email that appears to come from a valid organization, as a general rule legitimate organizations do not solicit funds through email. Despite how official an email may seem, it could very well be a scam. Many scams use the names of actual organizations and include a link to a website where you can make a donation. Do not follow any links within the message; these tend to be fake websites that are made to look like the organization's official site. Email solicitations may also include information about a foreign bank account where you can send your contribution. An organization requesting you to send funds to a foreign bank is *always* a sham.

9-11 set the criminal standard for using the Internet to take advantage of a crisis; every Internet-based scam was either used or originated from the 9-11 Internet frauds. Through relief scams, false charities and variations, cyber-hustlers literally used every trick in the book to dupe and steal from financial contributors worldwide when people were the most emotionally vulnerable. Not everyone walks into the well-laid traps of these Internet predators. 9-11, and the fraud that ensued, also awakened individuals to the dangerous world of scam artists outside of American borders as well as within their own broadband.[128]

The best course of action is this: *never* respond to unsolicited emails, commonly referred to as SPAM. Do not open any attachments to these emails even if they claim to contain pictures of a particular tragedy. These attachments are probably viruses that may allow hackers to gain access to your computer. If you are genuinely interested in donating to a charity, initiate contact directly with the organization. Investigate the organization's Web address or call them directly. Make sure you seek out the charity's authorized website and be on your guard, the results of a general Web search on Google, Yahoo! or another search engine may actually include a fraudulent site designed to look like a legitimate charity's website.

Charities and organizations may use people, animals or religious figures to lure in victims to participate. Some claim the money will be used to educate and feed poor children in another country or provide medical help. Charities or

---

[128] http://www.toptenz.net/top-10-charity-scams.php

organizations create commercials or articles demonstrating how important donations are to the success of that group's mission. Other organizations claim that donations are needed to increase the life span of an endangered species. Pictures of the endangered animal are shown to create a selling opportunity by appealing to your emotions.[129]

Following the 2005 devastation of the American Gulf Coast, the FBI estimates around 4,000 websites sprang up to misdirect genuine signs of charity into the bank accounts of shameless scammers. At least 60 percent of these were hosted on foreign servers, a move that generally sends up warning signs to anyone scanning for legitimacy. Some of the more egregious offenses solicited donations from the well-intentioned by posing as the Red Cross and other real charities doing real work—a sneaky strategy that worked before and, unfortunately, continued to do so.[130]

Social networking tools like Twitter, Facebook, YouTube and blogs deliver heart-wrenching images and information about charitable causes to our computers and phones. Many of them include pleas to donate. Television ads show us pictures of abused animals or starving children. While these methods can be powerful tools to inspire your desire to help, you should not blindly give because of a touching picture. Take the time to investigate the groups behind such pleas for help to ensure that it comes from a legitimate

[129] Laws.com blog, "Fraudulent Charities and Organizations At A Glance", http://fraud.laws.com/mail-fraud/fraudulent-charities-and-organizations

[130] Accounting Degree.com blog "The Top 9 Charity Scams of All Time", Aug 11, 2011, http://www.accountingdegree.com/blog/2011/the-top-10-charity-scams-of-all-time/

nonprofit, and then go to that charity's website to make your donation.

WHAT CAN YOU DO?

Don't give directly to anyone alleging to be a victim of a disaster. One thing that never changes: scammers follow the headlines—and the money. People affected by a disaster are in no position to contact you directly for assistance. Instead, find a charity with a proven track record of success with dealing with the type of disaster in the region in which the disaster occurred. Avoid fly-by-night charities created specifically to deal with a new crisis. Even well-meaning organizations created for that particular tragedy will not have the infrastructure to efficiently utilize your gift.

How can you determine if a site is valid? Start by examining the Web address. Most non-profit Web addresses end with .org and not .com. Avoid Web addresses that end in a series of numbers. Also, bogus sites often ask for detailed personal information such as your social security number, date of birth or your bank account and PIN information. Be extremely skeptical of these sites as providing this information makes it easy for them to steal your identity.

When you make a donation online, make sure you 'opt-out' and tell the charity that you do not want to have your personal information distributed to any other entity. Depending on the charity, you can 'opt-out' either by calling, writing to the charity or clicking a button to opt-out when making an online donation.[131]

The best way to protect yourself is to search out consumer and charity watchdog sites like the *Better Business Bureau*, *Charity Navigator* or *GuideStar,* which list nonprofits' official Web addresses as well as tax forms and financial data. The BBB also rates charities based on 20 standards of accountability including the structure of the board of directors and the transparency of financial data.[132]

You do not always have to be afraid to make a donation online, as millions of dollars in online contributions make it safely to charitable organizations, but you do need to be cautious and determine that you're giving to an established, reputable and honorable organization.

The Federal "do-not-call" legislation has allowed most Americans to finally enjoy dinner in peace without being hassled by unwanted phone calls from telemarketers. However, when Congress passed the do-not-call legislation, they exempted nonprofit organizations. Since most telemarketing firms have lost for-profit accounts as a result of these laws, many are now turning to nonprofit organizations for new business, and we still can't get a decent evening without interruption of telemarketers!

Here are some tips if you think you are interested in listening to a telemarketing pitch for a donation:

---

[131] Charity Navigator, http://www.charitynavigator.org/

[132] Ellin, Abby, Ibid

- **Find Out Who's Calling.** Many phone calls soliciting charitable donations come from for-profit professional telemarketers that keep a sizable portion of your donation for themselves and don't really care about the cause they're promoting. Find out if the person with whom you are speaking works for a telemarketing company or is a volunteer or employee of the charity itself. Remember that you have the right to end the phone call whenever you wish. You should never feel coerced into giving. And although you are still eligible to receive calls soliciting contributions after you've registered your phone number with the National Do Not Call Registry, you do have some recourse. If you receive a call from a third-party telemarketer on behalf of a charity (rather than the charity itself), then you can ask that firm to stop calling. If the telemarketing firm calls again soliciting for the same charity, then that firm could face a fine.[133]

- **Ask Where Your Donation Goes**. Professional, for-profit telemarketers typically negotiate their fees ahead of time and know exactly how much of every dollar raised goes to the charity and how much stays with the telemarketer. Companies often keep a significant portion of each dollar raised, and sometimes no money is returned to the charity. So be sure to ask the person on the other end of the line to

---

[133] Charity Navigator, Ibid

tell you how much of your donation will actually end up with the charity.

- **Get It In Writing**. Ask the person calling to send you a copy of the charity's annual report or a brochure describing its mission and accomplishments. Effective and efficient charities are proud of their accomplishments and are able to provide written materials describing their mission, program accomplishments, and financial information. Warning flags should go up if an organization refuses to send you a copy of their financial report or similar information; by law, all charities are required to provide financial and governance details to the public.[134]

- **Eliminate The Middle-Man**. If you determine that the telemarketer is calling you on behalf of a charity that you wish to support, contact the charity and find out how to donate to it directly. That way you avoid having part of your donation taken by a for-profit company.

- **Resist Giving Online to Police and Firefighters**. Most solicitations for police and fire service organizations are made by paid professional fund-raisers. Ask how your contribution will be used and what percentage of your contribution will go to the fire or police organization or program. You can also

---

[134] Golden Girl Finance blog, "Are celebrity charities too often a scam?", Money Media, February 8th, 2014 by Golden Girl Finance

call your local police or fire department to verify a fund-raiser's claim to be collecting on behalf of the organization or department. If the claim cannot be verified, report the solicitation to your local law enforcement officials. Be wary if a fund-raiser suggests you'll receive special treatment for donating and don't feel intimidated if you decline to give.

To help you determine which charities are committed to protecting your privacy, go to the Charity Navigator website. It has accountability and transparency evaluations including an assessment of each charity's donor privacy policy. To meet its criteria, a charity must have a written donor privacy policy that states it will not sell or trade the personal information of its donors. And that policy must be prominently displayed on the charity's website or in its marketing and solicitation materials.[135]

Another way to check up on a charity is to make sure the organization is a registered entity. Most states have registration and licensing rules that charities are required to abide by. In order to obtain tax-exempt status from the IRS (in the U.S.), an organization must file certain documents to prove their charitable operating procedure. The IRS provides information on these organizations via their Exempt Organizations Select Check tool.[136] Ask if your contribution is tax-deductible. Make your check payable to

---

[135] Charity Navigator, Ibid

[136] http://www.irs.gov/Charities-&-Non-Profits/Exempt-Organizations-Select-Check

the official name of the group or charity. Avoid cash gifts since cash can be lost or stolen.

Crooks use clever schemes to defraud millions of people every year. They often combine sophisticated technology with age-old tricks to get people to send money or to give out personal information under the guise of soliciting for a charity. They add new twists to old schemes and pressure people to make important decisions on the spot. The worst part about these scammers is that legitimate charities now face fierce competition from fraudsters, and the average person often doesn't know who to trust. Don't assume that most charitable organizations are corrupt, however. Most philanthropic organizations are working for very good causes and putting as much of the proceeds as they can towards making a lasting impact. At the end of the day, it's your due diligence that will weed out the worthy charities from the unscrupulous.

Chapter 8
The Plague of Medical Identity Theft

Edward Snowden, the former National Security Agency contractor who disclosed the agency's activities to the media, says the NSA has cracked the encryption used to protect the medical records of millions of Americans.[137]

MEDICAL IDENTITY THEFT

Medical identity theft is the misuse of a person's identity to obtain health care, either goods or services. Electronic medical record keeping is making this type of theft easier, and often the first time a person realizes he is a victim of medical identity theft is when he receives a statement from an insurance company for a treatment he didn't receive. "Medical identity theft has been called the privacy crime that can kill," said California Attorney General Kamala D. Harris. "This is because medical identity theft can corrupt medical records with erroneous information that can lead to incorrect diagnosis and treatment." [138]

Recently, the Identity Theft Resource Center produced a survey showing that medical-related identity theft

---

[137] Ollove, Michael, Ibid

[138] California Department of Justice, Office of the Attorney General, "Medical Identity Theft", https://oag.ca.gov/sites/all/files/agweb/pdfs/privacy/medical_id_theft_recommend.pdf

accounted for 43 percent of all identity thefts reported in the United States in 2013. That is a far greater chunk than identity thefts involving banking and finance, the government and the military or education. The U.S. Department of Health and Human Services says that since it started keeping records in 2009, the medical records of between 27.8 million and 67.7 million people have been breached.[139]

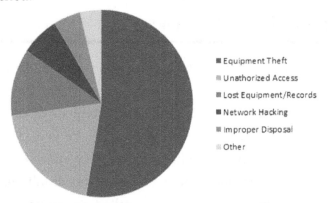

Medical Data Breaches (Chicago Tribune, Business Section 2, Aug. 29, 2013)

Victims sometimes discover erroneous information in their medical files during a doctor or hospital visit, and that may pose a bigger danger than the financial risks. The medical records may now contain vital information like blood type, allergies, prescription drug use or a history of disease that is completely incorrect. In an emergency, doctors could treat you based on this mistaken information.

When people are not aware their medical identities have been stolen, insurance companies may simply continue to

---

[139] Ollove, Michael, "The Rise Of Medical Identity Theft In Healthcare", *Kaiser Health News*, Feb. 7, 2014

pay the fraudulent claims without the victim's knowledge. The person might only learn of the fraud when trying to make a legitimate claim and the insurance company informs them they have reached their lifetime cap on benefits.[140] Even without your insurance information, if someone gets hold of your name and social security number, they can use them to receive emergency medical services, which many hospitals are obliged to provide.

> The largest U.S. medical data breach occurred in September 2011, when the vendor who operates Tricare, the health program for U.S. military members and their dependents, lost data on 4.9 million patients when back-up tapes were stolen from an employee's car.[141]

There are many ways that medical identity theft can be used by thieves such as using a victim's identity to obtain prescription drugs like Valium or obtaining medical treatment for themselves under a false insurance card.

For example, in one case a Seattle woman discovered that her newborn son's social security number had been stolen when she received a bill addressed to her son from a clinic prescribing him OxyContin for a work-related back injury.[142]

---

[140] Konrad, Walencia, "Your Medical Problems Could Include Identity Theft", *New York Times*, Jun 12, 2009

[141] Frost, P, "Feds, State target data theft", *Chicago Tribune*, Aug. 29, 2013, Business Section pg. 3

[142] "The Imposter in the ER: Medical identity theft can leave you with hazardous errors in your medical records", *MSNBC*, www.msnbc.msn.com/id/23392229

One way for medical information to be stolen is by insiders at a medical office. Thieves download vital personal insurance data and related information from the operation's computerized medical records, then sell it on the black market or use it themselves to make fraudulent billing claims.[143]

Another way is by unscrupulous hackers who break into medical record systems and steal data to sell to someone who will use it to target thousands of patients. With this type of data, criminals can set up fake provider identifications and fraudulently bill insurance companies or the government through Medicare. They can also use the stolen social security numbers to obtain credit cards, lines of credit and false ID cards.

There are huge privacy implications if someone can find out if a person has a disease that they want to keep hidden. They could discover that a person has had an abortion, been treated for depression, spent time in a mental institution, had HIV/AIDS or a venereal disease. This type of information can be used for blackmail, particularly if it is about a well-known celebrity or political figure. Also vulnerable in medical records is information concerning marital status, family, employment and other parts of a person's life.

Medical identity theft has been under-reported because it is difficult to detect, but it is a significant problem. In a 2008 report, the U.S. Department of Health and Human Services

---

[143] Konrad, Walencia, Ibid

estimated the number of victims at half a million, but since then the Ponemon Institute calculated that there were 1.84 million victims in 2013 alone—a 21 percent increase over the previous year. They also estimated that the costs incurred by U.S. victims were $12.3 billion.[144]

Knowledge that the crime is increasing has not, however, increased the means for preventing, detecting and remedying the problem. Regrettably, victims lack rights and resources comparable to those available to address financial identity theft. Experts agree that those rights and resources should include free annual access to records, flags on compromised identities, easy access to records suspected of containing fraudulent information and prompt correction of information resulting from fraud.[145]

Insurance companies advise that if you believe someone is using your health insurance, speak to your health insurance provider's fraud department to report the misuse. Removing the false information is just as important as clearing up any charges—insurance companies could charge you higher rates or reject you based on a medical identity thief's health history. And information about the identity thief's medical history, noted in charts as your own if the thief obtained medical care in your name, could lead to life-threatening mistakes in your medical care. This is especially true in an emergency situation when you may not be

---

[144] "2013 Survey on Medial Identity Theft", Ponemon Institute, Sept. 2013, www.ponemon.org

[145] California Department of Justice, Ibid

conscious or otherwise able to correct false information in your medical files.

> A suburban Chicago hospital network has announced that four computers containing unencrypted personal information for more than four million patients had been stolen in 2013. The theft occurred during a burglary at its administrative offices, and the computers contained names, addresses, dates of birth and social security numbers. Now federal regulators are investigating, and the group admits that medical data for some patients is at risk, including treating physicians and/or departments, diagnoses, medical record numbers, medical record service codes and health insurance information.[146]

In the case above, the compromised Chicago hospital network first claimed that the computers did not contain medical records and that they had waited to disclose the theft because they wanted to do an internal audit to see what data was on the computers and identify the affected patients. Later, the hospital disclosed on their website that their investigation confirmed the computers contained patient information used by them for administrative purposes and may have included patient demographic information and limited clinical information. After the fact, the hospital group stated, "We deeply regret that this incident has occurred. In order to prevent such an incident from reoccurring, we have enhanced our security measures and are conducting a thorough review of our policies and procedures." This medical group has about 1,000 doctors at more than 200 hospitals, and the records included anyone who had visited a medical group doctor. They admitted

---

[146] Placek, Christopher, "Personal Data of 4 million Advocate patients stolen", NW Daily Herald, Aug 23, 2003, https://www.dailyherald.com

they had poor security measures and no encryption of the data. [147]

DATA BROKERS AND YOUR MEDICAL INFORMATION

Federal law protects the confidentiality of your medical records and your conversations with your doctor. There are also strict rules regarding the sale of information used to determine your credit-worthiness or your eligibility for employment, your insurance and housing. Other than these certain kinds of protected data—including medical records and data used for credit reports—consumers have no legal right to control or even monitor how information about them is bought and sold.

As the FTC notes, "There are no current laws requiring data brokers to maintain the privacy of consumer data unless they use that data for credit, employment, insurance, housing, or other similar purposes." You may think from this statement that data brokers don't sell information about your health, but they do. Data companies can capture information about your "interests" in certain health conditions based on what you buy—or what you search for online. Datalogix has lists of people classified as "allergy sufferers" and "dieters." Acxiom sells data on whether an individual has an "online search propensity" for a certain "ailment or prescription." Credit reporting giant Experian has a separate marketing services division, which sells lists

---

[147] Placek, Christopher, Ibid

of names of expectant parents and families with newborns that are "updated weekly".[148]

Consumer data is also beginning to be used to evaluate whether you're making healthy choices. One health insurance company bought data on more than three million people's consumer purchases in order to flag health-related actions like purchasing plus-sized clothing. Spokeswoman Michelle Douglas said that BlueCross BlueShield of North Carolina would use the data to target free programming offers to their customers. Douglas suggested that it might be more valuable for companies to use consumer data "to determine ways to help me improve my health" rather than "to buy my data to send me pre-paid credit card applications or catalogs full of stuff they want me to buy."[149]

The *Wall Street Journal* has found many tracking files that collect sensitive health data. On Encyclopedia Britannica Inc.'s dictionary website Merriam-Webster.com, one tracking file from Healthline Networks Inc., an ad network, scans the page a user is viewing and targets ads related to what it sees there. So, for example, a person looking up depression-related words could see Healthline ads for depression treatments on that page—and on subsequent pages viewed on other sites. Healthline says it doesn't let advertisers track users around the Internet who have

---

[148] Beckett, Lois, "Everything we Know About What Data Brokers Know About You," *Propublica,* https://www.propublica.org/article/everything-we-know-about-what-data- brokers-know-about-you

[149] Angwin, Julia, "The New Goldmine, Your Personal Data and Tracking Online", *Wall Street Journal,* July 30, 2010

viewed sensitive topics such as HIV/AIDS, sexually transmitted diseases, eating disorders and impotence. But the company does let advertisers track people with bipolar disorder, overactive bladder and anxiety, according to its marketing materials.[150]

Even huge insurers like BlueCross BlueShield share your information. In their Privacy Notice, they state that they receive and use nonpublic personal financial information that you provide to them and that they gather from your insurance application. They also receive this information from consumer reporting agencies, from your health care claims, your payment information and customer service inquiries. They share this information with their company affiliates, insurance brokers, banks, reinsurers, other insurers, clinical programs and the business partners that provide services on their behalf—including marketing. Quite a long list, but that's not all: they also provide your information to regulatory agencies, law enforcement agencies, other governmental entities and to the military and NSA.[151]

The list goes on. They can share your information to help with public health and safety issues such as:

1. Preventing disease

2. Helping with product recalls

3. Reporting adverse reactions to medications

---

[150] Angwin, Julia, Ibid

[151] BlueCross BlueShield of Illinois Privacy Statement, Sept 1, 2013, Page 1

4. Reporting suspected abuse, neglect or domestic violence

5. Preventing or reducing a serious threat to anyone's health or safety

6. Reporting on worker's compensation claims

7. Responding to a court order or subpoena.

OTHER MEDICAL PRIVACY CONCERNS

Genetic testing is a new area that is raising some privacy concerns. People who want to know if they have inherited a risk factor for certain kinds of diseases are able to unlock secrets from their DNA for affordable sums ranging from $100 to $3500. A law passed in 2008 prevents health insurers from using genetic information against you, and employers can't use it either. But federal law doesn't offer the same protection for long-term-care, life insurance and disability coverage. The concern is that insurance companies could require you to show certain medical records or even just ask if you've had DNA testing.[152]

The Affordable Care Act has caused some privacy unease because of the information you are forced to give, such as social security number and W2 information, which can be shared among many government agencies, including the IRS, Social Security Administration and Department of Homeland Security. However, the Act has escalated the

---

[152] Lee, Anne "Cracking Open Your Own Code", *CNN Money*, Apr. 2013, pg. 51

migration to electronic medical records, and it is hoped that this will curtail medical identity theft.

YOUR PRIVACY RIGHTS UNDER HIPPA

HIPAA (Health Insurance Portability and Accountability Act) was originally enacted in 1996. In 2003, the part of the Act relevant to privacy directed the Department of Health and Human Services to write a health privacy rule. HIPAA gives each patient some rights, but HIPAA also permits uses and disclosures of health records without the patient's consent. Many will find some of these uses and disclosures objectionable because a patient doesn't have the opportunity to control the disclosure of his or her records. Our health care system—with third-party payers and lots of government involvement (e.g., Medicare and public health)—places many demands on health records. The number of government and private institutions that can ask for and receive health records without your permission numbers in the tens of thousands.[153] And with only a few exceptions, these government agencies can make nearly all permissible uses and disclosures without your consent, and they can even make them over your express written objection.

Everyone wants low-cost, high-quality health care for all but achieving this objective often affects privacy in negative ways. The trade-offs can be harsh, and HIPAA is decidedly

---

[153] A Patient's Guide to HIPAA "Learning About HIPAA", World Privacy Forum, Part 1, http://www.worldprivacyforum.org/2013/09/hipaaguidepart1/

a mixed bag for privacy. It does some good things and some not-so-good things. It protects privacy rights in some ways and undermines those rights in other ways at the same time.[154]

There is a new right to restrict disclosure of health information under the updated HIPAA health privacy rule. The new provision, called "Pay Out of Pocket" and also called the "Right to Restrict Disclosure," gives patients the right to request that their health care provider not report or disclose their information to their health plans when they pay for medical services in full. Navigating the new right will take effort and planning for patients to utilize this provision effectively and only covers those who do not use insurance but pay their own bill and the new right has several prerequisites. A patient has the firm right to demand that a health care provider not disclose the patient's protected health information to the patient's health plan if these conditions are met:

1. The patient makes a Request to Restrict disclosure;

2. The disclosure is to a health plan for payment or health care operations;

3. The disclosure is not required by law, and

4. The protected health information pertains solely to health care for which the patient (or someone on

---

[154] *World Privacy Forum*, Ibid

behalf of the patient) has paid for in full out of pocket.[155]

Many question whether this new law will even help patients since only a few people can afford to pay for their own care. For most patients, the right will be unavailable. Another wrinkle is that a patient who pays for his own care may not be able to negotiate a lower price like health plans often pay. If a person is on Medicare, this will prohibit providers taking any payment from some patients, so the option may not be available when a patient on Medicare uses outside providers. The same goes for HMOs; payments by patients for some services are not allowed even if service came from someone outside the HMO network.

CHILDREN'S PRIVACY RIGHTS

The Privacy Rule of HIPPA generally allows a parent to have access to the medical records about his or her child as his or her minor child's personal representative when such access is not inconsistent with state or other law.

There are three situations when the parent would not be the minor's personal representative under the Privacy Rule:

1. When the minor is the one who consents to care and the consent of the parent is not required under state or other applicable law;

---

[155] Gellman, Bob & Dixon, Pam, "Paying Out of Pocket to Protect Health Privacy", *World Privacy Forum*, *http://www.worldprivacyforum.org/2014/01/wpf-report-paying-out-of-pocket-to-protect-health-privacy/*

2. When the minor obtains care at the direction of a court or a person appointed by the court; and

3. When, and to the extent that, the parent agrees that the minor and the health care provider may have a confidential relationship.

However, even in these exceptional situations, the parent may have access to the medical records of the minor related to this treatment when state or other applicable law requires or permits such parental access. On the other hand, a provider may choose not to treat a parent as a personal representative when the provider reasonably believes, in his or her professional judgment, that the child has been or may be subjected to domestic violence, abuse or neglect, or that treating the parent as the child's personal representative could endanger the child.[156]

Basically the law states that if a child has a right to make a health care decision about himself or herself, then the child has the right to control information associated with that decision. Otherwise, a parent or guardian or a personal representative can exercise privacy rights on behalf of a child.

WHAT CAN YOU DO?

BlueCross BlueShield, and all health insurance companies, send a notice of your rights to information and of their

---

[156] U.S. Department of Health and Human Services, "Personal Representatives and Minors", http://www.hhs.gov/hipaafaq/personal/227.html

responsibilities. Here are typical things that you should absolutely consider and perhaps act upon:[157]

1. Get a copy of your health and claims records. (They may charge a fee.)

2. Ask your insurance company to correct health and claims records if you think they are incorrect or incomplete.

3. Ask to limit what the insurance company shares. You can ask they *not* share certain of your health information for treatment or payment.

4. Obtain a list of those with whom the insurance company has already shared information.

5. File a complaint with the U.S. Department of Health and Human Service Office for Civil Rights if you feel an insurance company has violated your privacy rights.

6. State laws may provide additional protection on some specific medical conditions or health information. For example, these laws may prohibit an insurance company from disclosing or using information related to HIV/AIDS, mental health, alcohol or substance abuse and genetic information without the insured's authorization.

---

[157] BlueCross BlueShield of Illinois "Your Information, Your Rights, Our Responsibilities", Sep 23, 2013

7. It is the responsibility of the insurance company to notify a person promptly if a breach occurs that compromises protected health information.

Other things you can personally do include asking your medical provider if your information is encrypted. In many data thefts from medical offices, the data was not. Most people do not want to change doctors, but do you really want to continue to visit a medical office where your information can easily be stolen or hacked?

You need to keep accurate records of all medical and hospital treatments because if you do have to correct your records due to medical identity theft, it can take a long time, and you won't remember everything that happened if you do not write it all down. Your records may also be important if you ever file a lawsuit over a case of medical identity theft or if you need to correct errors that may be in your health files.

You should be cautious in signing an authorization for additional disclosure of your information. Ask your provider what is the purpose for the disclosure and look to see if that purpose is properly described. Is it only for another physician who may be treating you, or is the authorization for your employer to explain your absence from work? If for your employer, you may want to be sure that the authorization only covers your recent illness and not treatment from the past. Will the disclosure reveal information to an insurance company that you don't want to reveal and don't have to share? Is this disclosure for a marketing activity? If so, you might not want to sign it. And make sure the disclosure has an expiration date and does not cover future illnesses.

If you believe your insurance card has been stolen or someone is using your health insurance, notify your health insurance provider's fraud department. If you wish to file a complaint you can do so with the U.S. Department of Health and Human Services Office for Civil Rights at www.hhs.gov/privacy/hipaa/complaints/ or by calling them at 1-877-696-6775. To obtain a full text of HIPA rules, go to: http://www.hhs.gov/ocr/privacy/hipaa/ administrative/combined/hipaa-simplification-201303.pdf.

Most of the responsibility for preventing medical identity theft lies with the healthcare industry, and strategic use of technology mandated under the Affordable Care Act is aimed at preventing the loss or misuse of patient records.

If you are receiving Medicare, you should write to your congressman asking him to support the new bipartisan "Preventing and Reducing Improper Medicare and Medicaid Expenditures Act of 2013" — known as the PRIME Act — which would combat fraud. Specifically, the PRIME Act would:

1. Prevent Medicare thieves from pretending to be doctors by curbing the use of stolen physician identities

2. Stiffen penalties for identity theft and outlaw the fraudulent purchase, sale or distribution of Medicare and Medicaid beneficiary ID numbers

3. Improve rewards for fraud tips and engage more Medicare beneficiaries in the fight against fraud

4. Crack down on improper billing (almost $30 billion in the Medicare pay-for-service program in 2012 alone) by requiring Medicare to more closely track overpayments and implement solutions to address them

5. Penalize the private bill-paying companies (which reimburse providers) that overpay providers and do not meet specific payment accuracy goals.[158]

Medical identity theft is a subset of health care fraud, but it is more than just a crime against the health care system. Medical identity theft can also have financial and other life-threatening consequences for patients. This is a crime involving theft and abuse of identity information that places individual victims at a risk. You can cancel your credit card but you can't cancel assaults on your body by medical misdiagnosis and erroneous, even deadly, treatment.

---

[158] Rand, Barry, "Pass the PRIME Act", *AARP Bulletin*, Sept 2013, pg. 36

Chapter 9
Will Your Digital Assets Be Buried?

When their youngest son died unexpectedly, the parents looked to his Facebook account for some comfort. The family felt that as the heirs to their son's estate, they were entitled to access his digital assets, including his social media accounts, email, digital photos and online banking records. However, Facebook refused to give them access, and despite a court fight, Facebook has continued its policy of not turning over the account.[159]

DIGITAL ASSETS

First, we need to define *digital assets*. One definition commonly used states that a digital asset is any item of text or media that has been formatted into a binary source that includes the right to use it. A digital file without the right to use it is not an asset. Digital assets are categorized into three major groups, which may be defined as textual content (digital assets), images (media assets) and multimedia (also media assets).[160] You can also take a more legal approach and define digital assets as files and digital accounts and the access rights to those files. Evan Carroll, co-author of *Your Digital Afterlife*, states, "The term digital assets means, but is

---

[159]CNBC News, "Mother fights for access to her deceased son's Facebook account", *Associated Press*, Mar 1, 2013

[160] van Niekerk, A.J., "The Strategic Management of Media Assets", Allied Academies, New Orleans Congress, 2006

not limited to, files, including, but not limited to, emails, documents, images, audio, video, and similar digital files which currently exist or may exist...including, but not limited to, desktops, laptops, tablets, peripherals, storage devices, mobile telephones, Smartphones, and any similar digital device which currently exists or may exist as technology develops...regardless of the ownership of the physical device upon which the digital asset is stored."[161]

None of us should think that our digital assets are unimportant since they may be very valuable to heirs once we are gone. Another way to look at it is that digital assets are anything with a sentimental or financial value that you can't hold in your hand. It could be a record of reward points earned from your hotel stays, online photos of your children, credit card accounts, stock and commodity trading accounts or simply a list of favorite poems.

Data sets that can be inherited can include instructive memos, digital contracts, digital receipts, pictures, intellectual property, medical files and financial information. In 2012, United States shoppers spent around $600 million buying digital films and TV shows and another $7 billion on iTunes. Flickr, the digital photo album, stores more than six billion photos. One in four books is now an e-book bought from Kindle, Nook or Apple's iBooks.[162]

---

[161] Carroll, Evan & Romano, John, "When Flickr and Twitter are Your Estate, What's Your Legacy?", New Riders, Nov. 25, 2010

[162] Carroll, Evan, Digital Estate Resource, Jan. 2012

Data heirs are faced with so much data that they are often unable to separate the nice-to-have assets from crucial or core assets. Another problem is posed by the fact that many contracts with service providers are automatically terminated (by the terms of service) as soon as the customer ceases to exist.

It is not unreasonable to assume that a family may want to look through emails or a Facebook account if a person dies or is killed unexpectedly, whether in an accident or military service. However, some civil liberties groups say it's not always obvious what someone would want to share. Experts say that online companies craft their privacy agreements to keep the contents of user accounts private after death or disability in cases where a person has not given explicit permission to share an account.

A recently published case from the Massachusetts Appeals Court, Ajemian v. Yahoo!, deals with the unfortunate difficulties of administrators gaining access to their deceased loved one's email accounts. Yahoo!'s contention in the Ajemian case is that the Stored Communications Act prohibits them from disclosing the contents of an email user's account. Next of kin are facing this issue more and more since social media accounts have strong privacy policies.[163] (See pg. 159 for Stored Communications Act.)

By some estimates, nearly a half a million people with Facebook accounts passed away last year, leaving family

---

[163] Goldman, Eric, "Yahoo's User Agreement Fails in Battle Over Dead User's Email Account–Ajemian v. Yahoo", *Technology & Marketing Law blog.* May 9, 2013, ericgoldman.org/archives/2013/05

and friends to decide what to do with those pages. Leave the account open? Shut it down entirely? Convert it to an official Facebook memorial page?[164]

GAINING ACCESS TO DIGITAL ACCOUNTS

Despite the various online sites making it difficult to obtain digital assets, it's essential to include online accounts in the estate-planning process. Failure to plan ahead may prevent loved ones from recovering family photos or videos or from settling your final bills. It also could leave your estate vulnerable to post-mortem identity theft if hackers decide to apply for credit cards in your name while nobody's watching your accounts. What's more, a library of digital music or an Internet domain name that you own may have financial value that's significant to your estate. Much of an individual's life now appears online, including bills, e-book accounts, movie collections, blogging sites and photo-sharing websites. Let's explore what happens to some of those digital assets when a person dies.

Under pressure, social media companies have started to implement processes whereby account holders can indicate preferences if they are out of action for a period of time. Google has announced a feature called "Inactive Account Manager." Users of services like Gmail, Picasa or YouTube can go to their settings and tell Google what to do after their account is inactive for a certain amount of time, like three or six months. Google will terminate the holdings of the

---

[164] Rosen, Rebecca, "The Government Would Like You to Write a 'Social Media Will'", *The Atlantic*, May 3, 2012, http://www.theatlantic.com

account, if requested, or have the data sent to specified contacts.

Previously, getting access to a deceased person's Gmail account required a death certificate, months of review and a court order—and likely still will, if the user doesn't take advantage of the Inactive Account Manager feature. This feature allows individuals to designate up to ten relatives or friends as their online account beneficiaries, and they can specify what they want to happen service by service.

Other providers differ on how they handle the accounts of deceased users, but some are starting to help users plan their digital afterlife. The Yahoo! terms of service, for example, say that "any rights to your Yahoo! ID or contents within your account terminate upon your death," and accounts may be deleted if a death certificate is submitted.

At Facebook, relatives now may be able to request the contents of the account—a lengthy process involving a court order—or ask that the page be deleted. A Facebook account can be "memorialized," meaning friends can still post messages on the page but no one can log in to the account. Some people think this can be comforting to the family to see that the messages continue and to realize people remember their loved one, but other people may not want a reminder of the person they lost by constantly having well-meaning people post messages and condolences.[165]

---

[165] Facebook Help Center, Report a Deceased Person, https://www.facebook.com/help/

DEALING WITH DEATH AND INCAPACITY

> James suffered a stroke. He ran a building supply business and kept all of his records, including his accounts receivable, in a Yahoo! account. His family, already coping with his stroke, tried to get access to the company emails but Yahoo! refused. Material was coming into the warehouse, but for whom? James finally awoke from a coma but couldn't remember his password or his "secret" questions, and Yahoo!, true to their privacy policy, wouldn't tell the family the password over the phone. He never did recover his password and his business took a big hit financially.[166]

Dealing with the broader world of death and incapacity is a prime objective of the Uniform Law Commission (ULC), a nonprofit association.[167] Attorneys appointed by state governments have been working under the group's umbrella on a digital-assets bill, trying to circumvent the "non-transferrable" problem by stating that giving access to a legal representative doesn't count as a transfer when the owner has passed on or if he becomes incapacitated in some way and needs help with his affairs. ULC Commissioner Suzy Walsh emphasizes that the process takes time, partly because they want input from as many affected parties as possible. She has stated that "it became clear that the social media folks are very uncomfortable with" incapacity provisions like letting a court-appointed caretaker manage an account for a mentally-disabled adult. Groups like the American Civil Liberties Union have weighed in on the

---

[166] Prangley, Karin, "The Disposition of Digital Assets: Estate Planning", *KSC Law*, 2012, www.ksc-law.com/publications/karin-c-prangley

[167] Beyer, Gerry, "Uniform Law Commission Helps Move Digital Asset Legislation", *Law Professors Blog Network*, Jun 7, 2013

process too, citing privacy concerns. And the ULC law won't deal with copyright-protected material. For example, the iTunes service agreement doesn't mention death of an account owner, and Apple does not have a policy on whether someone can inherit an account, with or without a will. [168]

At this writing, only seven states have estate laws that deal specifically with digital assets. In Connecticut, Rhode Island, Oklahoma, Indiana, Virginia, Nevada and Idaho, the law specifies what is and is not included in an estate. Other states have narrow laws that apply mainly to the assets of a minor, reflecting the nature of recent controversies about digital assets, which often involve service providers and parents who have lost children.

PREPARING A POWER OF ATTORNEY OR WILL

It is very important in this age of digital assets that your survivors know what you want. If you are uncomfortable with someone reading your email after you are gone, then you should specifically state in your will or power of attorney, "My parents/spouse/children cannot read my email after I die." However, you may want certain people to be able to read your correspondence, access your iTunes and candid snapshots, or have your passwords for online accounts. In this case, you need to think of including instructions in your will and determining which person or people should take charge when you are gone.

---

[168] Walsh, Suzy, "Some States Creating Digital Passing Laws Despite ULC's Work in Progress", *Estate Dispatch*, estatedispatch.com

It should be standard practice for attorneys to advise clients to include digital assets in their estate plans, but not many have been doing so. Consequently, it may be up to you to ask your attorney about including your assets in your will or estate plan, as well as whether you want to give an agent or executor the power to access your accounts.

If you wish to give an executor power to access or manage your online accounts, you can structure your will to read something like the following, but be aware that laws vary by state and you would be well-advised to consult an attorney about the wording for your particular will.

"My executor shall have the power to access, handle and dispose of my digital assets, and shall have the power to obtain, access, modify, delete and control my passwords and other electronic credentials associated with my digital devices and digital assets. My digital assets include, but are not limited to [modify this list for your particular assets]:

1. Files stored on my desktops, laptops, tablets, mobile telephones, Smartphones, blogs, peripherals, storage devices and any other similar digital device.

2. Digital music, digital photographs, digital videos, gaming accounts, social network accounts and file sharing accounts.

3. Email accounts and emails saved.

4. Software licenses, financial accounts, banking accounts, investment accounts, domain registrations, Web hosting accounts, tax

preparation service accounts, online store accounts, reward accounts, affiliate programs and similar digital assets which exist or may exist in the future, regardless of the physical device upon which the digital items are stored."

If you wish to grant another person access to your accounts, you may include a statement such as this sample:

"I authorize my executor to grant named person access to my digital assets so that they can handle or dispose of my digital assets according to a memorandum which I have prepared and which I may alter as I acquire or dispose of these assets. My executor and named person should follow my instructions as outlined in the memorandum."

You then have the option to list which accounts you wish to have made available and which files you wish to have deleted. Sometimes a library of digital music or an Internet domain name that you own may have financial value that's significant to your estate. Domain names are the same as real estate on the Internet. Germs.com, for example, was on sale on the domain name marketplace Sedo for $50,000. Many businesses spend millions of dollars on advertising just to promote their name in association with a specific product, so acquiring a good domain name is the equivalent of years of expensive advertising and marketing.[169]

"We shouldn't dismiss our digital assets as insignificant or unimportant," says Evan Carroll. "The things that may seem ephemeral to us are very valuable to heirs once we're gone."

---

[169] "The Value of Domain Names", Domain Gems, http://domaingems.com/value

[170] The value of these assets can go far beyond their financial worth in the wake of a loved one's death. As we said previously, having a Facebook account "memorialized," meaning friends can still post messages, photos, songs and holiday greetings can sometimes be comforting to the family to see the messages continue.

You might want to consider signing a statement authorizing the various online companies to disclose the contents of your accounts rather than having your executors try to access the accounts directly, perhaps violating the terms of service. For anyone writing a will or giving someone a power of attorney, here are some things to consider that will make it easier for your family:[171]

1. **Keep an inventory of what you have**. A digital asset is considered anything you access online. A few examples, in addition to your email and social medial accounts, may include digital photo albums or movie collections, a PayPal account, video game avatars, domain names, online subscriptions, online investment accounts, hotel or airline reward points and blogs. If you want your family to be able to access some or all of your digital assets, you will have to insure that someone has access to your passwords, user names and answers to security questions (and remember to update your inventory

---

[170] Carroll, Evan, Ibid

[171] Glorch, Robert, "Introduction to Estate Planning for Digital Assets", *Illinois Estate Plan*, Apr 21, 2013, http://www.illinoisestateplan.com/introduction-to-estate-planning-for-digital-assets/

if you change your passwords). You should put your inventory in a safe place and indicate in your will where it is located. If you want someone else to keep track of your inventory, there are quite a few commercial online sites that help you organize and keep track of your accounts and documents such as: organizemyaffairs.com, estatedocsorganizer.com, legacylocker.com, aftersteps.com, thedocsafe.com and safeboxfinancial.com.

2. **Research your state's laws or consult an attorney**. Seven states have laws that help representatives gain access to digital assets, and many more states have bills in the works. So far, those laws are far from uniform, and only these few states have attempted to clarify an executor's power when it comes to digital assets. Estate law, on the whole, also varies from state to state and is still catching up to the electronic world, which means that even if you meticulously plan, you may not be able bequeath your digital assets exactly as you would like. If you are unsure, consult an attorney who specializes in digital estate planning and research any new state laws.

3. **Identify the person who should be in charge of your digital assets**. This should definitely be someone you trust and someone who is computer literate. Make it clear who you want to have access to which assets, what valuables you want passed along to others, and which accounts you want shut down and deleted. If you want to give your online video collection or fantasy football league to your best

friend, for example, be sure that is spelled out in your will.

4. **Planning is also about your privacy**. If you don't specify what you want done with your email account and the executor has access, he will be able to read all your emails—even if you never wanted anyone else to see those private messages. That is especially true for those living in a state with a digital-asset law.

5. **Keep the list of usernames and passwords separate from the will**. Make a separate list with access information independent from the will and keep it in a safe place. This allows you to keep passwords updated and add new items easily—which is important given how often we add new accounts and/or change passwords. It is estimated that the average person has 25 password-protected accounts and will likely not be able to keep their "social-media wills" up to date on that many accounts. Also, because wills can become public documents, this helps guarantee that passwords stay private. There are companies, such as 1Password or LastPass, that will encrypt your log-in and password information and keep it stored on your own computer. You then have a master password to unlock all the data and, theoretically, you only have to keep one master password in your safe-deposit box or with your attorney.

6. Review those terms of service agreements that you never read. In spite of the time it takes, you should read through each online service provider's terms of service and see if you can transfer your account and/or give your password to your heirs. Most, such as Facebook and Gmail, have their own policies for handling accounts after a user dies.

> Even when family members have shared all their passwords with each other, managing online accounts can be difficult. Laura had all of her husband's passwords when he died in 2010, but she didn't have all of the log-in IDs he used for online bill payments. She tried to convert the online bills back to paper statements, which wasn't an easy process. Her electricity was turned off after the power company was slow to send her the paper bill that she had requested.[172]

SERVICE AGREEMENTS

- Facebook's terms of service says it will not issue login and password information to family members of a person who has died. A family member can contact Facebook and request the dead person's profile be taken down or turned into a memorial page. If the family chooses a memorial page, the account can never again be logged into. Alternately, Facebook will provide the estate of the deceased with a download of the account's data—if prior consent is obtained from

---

[172] Kiplinger, "Protect Digital Assets After Your Death", *NASDAQ*, Apr. 25, 2013 http://www.nasdaq.com/article/protect-digital-assets-after-your-death-cm240446#ixzz2daBOW3YQ

or decreed by the deceased or is mandated by law.

- Google's Gmail policy offers a two-step process wherein they *may* allow certain people access to a deceased person's account. If you have data stored on YouTube or Google accounts, you can now use Google's Inactive Account Manager to be sure your digit assets go to the person you want to inherit them. This new feature allows you to give your consent to transfer emails, photos and other data to an authorized executor. They will then mail the estate holder a CD with the decedent's account information after the beneficiary of the estate sends the required information. Users can also elect to have their data automatically deleted, or they can add up to ten people to a contact list to receive Gmail messages and data from other Google services, including Blogger, Google+, Picasa and YouTube. Google will send users a warning, either by cell phone or by emailing a secondary address, before taking any action when a pre-determined period of time has elapsed. The feature is now included on the Google Account settings page.

- Hotmail's policy requires a significant amount of information and paperwork—everything from photo ID of the executor to the approximate date of account creation and last login.

- <u>Yahoo!</u> says emails are private no matter what. Yahoo! also owns <u>Flickr</u> and says users can transfer accounts if they leave their consent and the password. Without those, survivors can only ask that the contents of an account be deleted.

- <u>Amazon (Kindle)</u> says books can be willed but there may be some issues since books are often licensed. It is much better to leave someone your Kindle e-reader or Barnes & Noble Nook with the books downloaded on them.

- <u>Twitter</u> has a policy of working with an authorized person to deactivate a deceased member's account, but the authorized person must already know the user name and password. Here is the information you must provide to Twitter to have an account deactivated:

  o The username of the deceased user's Twitter account (e.g., @username or twitter.com/username)
  o A copy of the deceased user's death certificate
  o A copy of your government-issued ID (e.g., driver's license)
  o A signed statement including your relationship to the deceased user or their estate, action requested (e.g., 'please deactivate the Twitter account'), and a brief description of the details that evidence this account belongs to the deceased if the name

on the account does not match the name on death certificate.

- <u>Virtual Games</u> such as Farmville, World of Warcraft, and Grand Theft Auto. Most will not allow avatar sales and say their accounts are not transferable. With proper paperwork, (see the hoops Twitter makes you jump through) some will honor a player's request in a will.

- Domain registrar <u>Go Daddy</u> has an established protocol that allows for the transfer of domains within 24 hours if the paperwork is in order. For other domains, check the policy of the registrar.

- When you download a song from <u>iTunes</u>, you don't actually own the song; instead, you have purchased a license to use the download during your lifetime. You should read your agreement to determine what you can pass on to someone else.

For accounts that are important to you (and may not be legally classified as your property or as something transferrable), research the fine print. This will help you leave more informed instructions and prepare your representative to take on the company policy, if that's what you desire. Sadly, even if your family has your passwords, they may have no clear authority to manage the online accounts, retrieve bills or look at bank accounts because of the varying online user agreements and state laws regarding a deceased person. On the other hand, some accounts aren't much of a challenge for estate planners because they have clear procedures for transferring assets to beneficiaries. Only by reading your service agreements will you know which accounts may pose a problem.

Keep up to date, because new laws may change the way sites are addressing digital life after death. Policymakers are considering laws that will make it easier for heirs to access the accounts of the deceased and define the lines of ownership. Considering the amount of money spent on music, videos, gaming and e-books, legislators need to provide some guidance to the providers of these products. Otherwise buyers must realize that they are only renting these assets and that upon their death, the digital assets will revert back to the provider.

Currently, federal laws present another hurdle. If you use your late mother's password to log on to her account, you may violate not only the provider's terms of service, but also the federal Computer Fraud and Abuse Act, which governs certain unauthorized access to computers. And a federal privacy law, the Stored Communications Act, can limit providers' ability to share deceased users' account contents with relatives.[173]

The Stored Communications Act (SCA) is a law that addresses voluntary and compelled disclosure of "stored wire and electronic communications and transactional records" held by third-party Internet service providers (ISPs). Basically, it states that the Fourth Amendment privacy protections apply to information stored online and, in general, ISPs are forbidden to "divulge to any person or

---

[173] Kiplinger, Ibid

entity the contents of any communication which is carried or maintained on that service." It goes on to state, "The SCA provides criminal penalties for anyone who intentionally accesses without authorization, a facility through which an electronic communication service is provided."[174] The intent of the act was to stop criminal hacking, but it is now being used to prevent access to accounts by relatives after a person is deceased.

WHAT CAN YOU DO WITHOUT A WILL?

If you do not have a will, you can download some of your online account information to your home computer. Facebook will allow users to copy all of their correspondence, along with photographs, in a single download. There are also some companies that will download content from Facebook, Twitter, Gmail and others for you.

You can also create your own backup of your important files and deposit the backup offsite. This allows you to determine the person who will post-mortem distribute any or all data. If you decide to use this solution, be sure to also include a list of IDs and passwords for your online accounts.

Still another alternative is to buy a service that will transfer your digital assets to your heirs, but be aware that there may be potential conflicts with online providers' terms of service or federal laws. Jurisdiction can also be an issue.

---

[174] Wikipedia, Stored Communications Act

Since many companies have their servers located in different countries, this could mean that assets are subject to different probate legalities. For example, the country of domicile's law may be different from the country of origin, which could be problematic.[175]

It's important to be organized and in control—having a central repository where you make all your usernames and passwords available to your online executor will help ease the transfer of digital assets and the pain of your departure. But if you do want to investigate these companies, keep in mind before any money changes hands that the most secure method is to have your instructions in your will or power of attorney. If you choose to use one of the companies that offer options for passing on online account access after death, you may want to consider *Legacy Locker SecureSafe, Sourceforge, Keeper* or *My Webwill*, to name a few.

We all need to face the fact that we will probably not outlive our Facebook, Kindle, and iTunes accounts. People are just now realizing how much of their life is online and coming to grips with the fact that they not only have to think about who will inherit their tangible assets—like that antique desk, the diamond engagement ring, or those silver coins they put away for a rainy day—but also the less visible assets: those of their digital life.

You never know when that day will come, but in the meantime you would be wise to go through your accounts

---

[175] "Digital life after death: transfer of digital assets", *MSO.net*, May 28, 2013, http://www.mso.net/Digital-life-after-death-transfer-of-digital-assets

and delete old or unwanted files, store the photos you want to keep on thumb drives and decide if you really need to have online copies of old bills, tax returns and other outdated financial records. The more you have in cyberspace, the more there is for your family to sort through—not to mention the more there is for hackers to find.

Finally, having an online presence does not necessarily mean that you have electronic property that has value and that you need to consult an attorney. However, "value" means different things to different people. It may mean monetary value (such as a vast digital video library, a PayPal seller account or hundreds of thousands of airline miles), or it can mean sentimental value (such as digital photographs of your children or your carefully researched family tree). It is up to you to decide if you need to include these items in a will or simply let someone in your family know how to access them.

The Bank of America lost at least $10 million to criminals. About 95 members of the loosely affiliated criminal gang behind the alleged fraud, including a bank employee, had stolen names, addresses, social security numbers, phone numbers, bank account numbers, driver's license numbers, birth dates, email addresses, mother's maiden names, PINs and account balances. It appears that this information was then used for identity theft. According to one victim, quoted in an LA Times story, the scammers ordered boxes of checks and had them delivered to a UPS outlet where they would then pick them up. They also allegedly contacted the victim's telephone company and—to prevent Bank of America from warning the victim—re-routed calls to the scammers' mobile phone.[176]

ONLINE BANKING

Online banking is incredibly easy and convenient. But it does come with certain risks. Just as you hear of people being robbed at ATMs or having their cards cloned, online banking is also vulnerable. Banking websites are likely hit by hacking attacks every single day. While that may be unsettling to hear, if hackers do steal money from your account, you will be protected since banks are liable for any stolen funds. Banks are not liable, however, for the personal

---

[176] McMillan, Robert, "Insider data theft costs Bank of America $10 million", *Computer World*, May 25, 2011

information that a hacker might obtain, like your social security number, address, birth date and PIN.

The main issue people have with online banking is that of trust. They wonder if their transaction went through successfully or not. While the collection, storage and sharing of customer information is an important part of delivering banking products and services to consumers, the questions remain: How secure is online banking and the networks they use? How trustworthy are the people who handle the transactions? How easily can thieves hack into their systems? When you opened your online banking account, you received a privacy statement that read something like this one:

> We understand that you expect us to maintain proper safeguards to protect confidential information you provide to us. The privacy of your information is protected not only by state and federal laws, but by our commitment to the protection of your financial information. We have established policies and procedures to help prevent misuse of that information. This statement has been prepared to explain to you what types of information we collect, how we use that information, and the circumstances under which we may share all or part of that information. Under no circumstances do we provide deposit or loan account personal information to third parties for the purpose of independent telemarketing or direct mail marketing of any non-financial products or services of those companies. We disclose information permitted or required by a variety of federal and state laws, as required to consummate your transaction, and as directed by you. Our strict policies to protect your information apply equally to current (active) accounts as well as inactive (closed) accounts, both loans and deposits.[177]

---

[177] Copiah Bank Internet Privacy and Security Statement, www.copiahbank.com/about/online_security

And here is the important part: "For complete details of how we use your information, refer to our bank's PRIVACY POLICY". Just like other sites where we do business, how many of us actually take the time to read the documents that tell us who the bank shares information with—and how much they share?

WHAT DATA DO BANKS SHARE?

In most aspects of our lives, companies and marketers can freely collect details about us and sell them to whomever they like without restriction. Yet financial institutions, along with medical providers, are subject to U.S. laws limiting how they share our information. The U.S. Congress set limitations on financial institutions in the 1999 Gramm-Leach-Bliley Act.[178] A decade later, federal agencies mandated that banks explain how they use a client's personal data in a standardized privacy policy. Such rules make it easier to compare these practices than in many industries.

Lorrie Faith Cranor at Carnegie Mellon University thought it would be interesting to see if banks actually follow the law and see how they compare with each other. With help from her students, she analyzed 3,422 financial institutions. She found that practices vary widely, with many freely sharing some of our data, and 27 banks appearing to violate regulations on sharing information altogether.

---

[178] FDIC, "Privacy Act Issues under Gramm-Leach-Bliley", http://www.fdic.gov/consumers/consumer/alerts/glba.html

Some banks use your data to market to you directly or through affiliates. Some, including major players such as Bank of America, Citi, Capitol One, Chase, Discover Bank and HSBC, allow non-affiliated outside companies to market to you. These banks allow customers to opt out of such marketing—but you have to know it takes place and then go through all the trouble of figuring out how to opt out.[179]

As financial institutions seek to replace revenue that was cut under the Durbin Amendment[180]—part of the financial overhaul that limits the fees banks can charge retailers—they are exploring new business avenues including selling your data. New technologies are making these marketing channels increasingly plausible. [181]

BANKS FACE RISKS TOO

Most bank account thefts begin with a single malware developer who sells malicious software on an underground black market to hackers. Criminal hackers can buy tools to steal users' bank account credentials, services to bring down websites, or viruses to infect computers. Once unsuspecting victims' credentials or bank account information has been collected, hackers may resell that data to someone who

---

[179] Tanner, Adam, Ibid

[180] HR Simplified, "Durbin Amendment", http://hrsimplified.com/durbin-amendment-effective-april-1-2013/

[181] New, Catherine, "Beyond Card Fees: Banks Look To Sell Your Data", *Daily Finance*, Oct 25, 2011

repackages it in a useful way and redistributes it on the black market. [182]

Banks and financial institutions are facing an increased need to ensure their transactions are secure. Banks are most vulnerable to four common types of attacks that hackers use to steal information from them and other online merchants. These include:

- **Phishing**. This involves clicking on a fake Internet link to a page that looks like it was set up by your bank. The fake link could look almost identical to the bank's real homepage because the scammer has copied files from the real site. When searching for your bank on the Internet, you could get the fake site along with the real site and unknowingly click on the fake site. When you attempt to log in to your account, the site asks for information that the real site never would. It may ask not only for your name but also your account number, password, ATM PIN number or last digits of your debit card. Once you enter any of this sensitive data, the details are sent to the scammers. With your login details in hand—user name, password and personal identification number—they would be able to access your account and steal your money.

- **Identity theft**. Even if hackers don't steal from your account, they can capture your personal information,

---

[182] Lobosco, Katie "Cyberattacks are the bank robberies of the future", *CNN Money*, Jul 9, 2013, http://money.cnn.com/2013/07/09/technology/security/cybercrime-bank-robberies/

such as your social security number and other identifying data, and steal your identity. That data could be used to create new accounts in your name or to hack into your other accounts.

- **Keylogging.** If you access your online banking site on public networks such as Internet cafes or public Wi-Fi, there is a chance that you could fall prey to keylogging. Hackers load software onto public networks to record your keystrokes and get your account details.

- **Pharming.** This might be a little more difficult for hackers to carry out, but it does happen. Pharming occurs when hackers are able to hijack a bank's URL so that when you try to access your bank's website, you get redirected to a bogus site that looks like the real thing. Once you access the bogus website, they have free rein to capture your account number, logon id, password and personal information.

A 2012 report revealed that close to 29% of all Internet users worldwide and 45% of Internet users in the North America, have accessed online banking sites. This represents roughly 423.5 million people.

As use of online banking expands, it has become an increasingly attractive target for hackers. In 2011, Citigroup revealed that more than 360,000 accounts were compromised in a hacking attack that left 3,400 accounts suffering losses of up to $2.7 million. Reuters reported that Iranian hackers had been targeting Citigroup, Bank of America and JPMorgan Chase with "denial of service" campaigns, making it difficult for customers to access their accounts.[183]

Denial-of-service attacks can be very disruptive because if a bank's website is repeatedly shut down, the attacks can hurt its reputation, affect customer retention and cause revenue losses when customers cannot open accounts or conduct other business.

> Barclay PLC and the U.K. banking regulator have launched investigations into allegations that information about thousands of the bank's customers was stolen and sold to brokers. In the past, the U.K. regulator has fined banks for losing control of customer data. In 2010, a U.K. insurance unit of Zurich Financial Services was fined £2.27 million ($3.7 million) for losing the details of 46,000 customers. HSBC Holdings was fined around £3.2 million over a similar issue in 2009, when staff lost a compact disk containing thousands of customer records.[184]

Hacker attacks raise concerns about the safety and security of our online banking transactions. It is equally important for bank clients to secure their equipment themselves. Hackers, like all other predators, will attack the weakest link. Should you pay your bills online? Should you check your balance from your bank's website? Should you transfer funds online? Yes, but use the same caution as you do with any other Internet site. Do not click links on emails or

---

[183] Finkle, Jim & Rothacker, Rick, "Iranian hackers target Bank of America, JPMorgan, Citi", *Reuters*, Sept 21, 2012

[184] Colchester, Max, "Barclays Probes Allegations of Data Theft", *Wall Street Journal*, Feb. 9, 2014

download anything from people you do not know or even from people you do know if the subject line looks dubious.

WHAT CAN YOU DO?

First, confirm your online bank's legitimacy. The Federal Deposit Insurance Corp. has a tool that lets you search for banks whose deposits it insures. It is very easy to do this: go to the FDIC website, www.fdic.gov[185], and look on the home page for an option that says "Bank Find." Clicking on the link will take you to a page where you can type in your bank's name and find out if it is FDIC insured. Also available at this site are the bank's locations and history.

Be alert to the possibility of copycat websites. Be sure you do not fall prey to sites that use a name that is very similar to that of your online bank—for example, BankofAnerica.com or Citigrop.com. Misspellings in emails supposedly from your bank are a dead giveaway that the email isn't legitimate. When you receive an email purporting to be from your bank, don't click any links in the email. Instead, type in the URL of your bank in the address field of your browser and then log in when the site comes up. If your bank is really trying to contact you, you'll likely find a message when you access your account. You can also call the number on the back of your credit card or on your latest bank statement.

Learn more about your bank's security system. You should know how your bank encrypts your private information.

---

[185] Bank Find, http://www2.fdic.gov

When you are accessing the website, you should find a small lock or key icon to tell you that the site and your transactions are secure. You should be required to use PINs and passwords when you access your account online.

Finally, do not send personal information over email. Under no circumstances would your bank ask for personal data via email.

The most important way of protecting your Internet banking transaction is by using a user ID and password that you select. Be sure to keep them a secret. Try to memorize them and, if you need to maintain a written record of the codes, store them away from your computer in a secure place, not in your wallet, purse or Smartphone.

If your computer is left unattended and the browser is running with your user ID and password entered, anyone can gain access to your accounts. Lock your computer when you need to leave it. Change your password often; make it difficult to figure out. Do not use simple words or numbers in sequence. It is recommended that you use upper case and lower case letters along with numbers and symbols that are unique to you. Stay away from the obvious words and numbers like a family member's birthday or name.

Protect your computer. Hacking attacks are not always directed at banks. Because many such attacks are directed at customers, you should have the latest virus and malware scanning software installed on your computer. You should also ensure that all the software you use on your computer has the latest security updates.

You should never get lazy when it comes to online banking. Some banking websites have an option that offers to "remember me on this computer." Choosing this option would allow you to bypass some security questions if the bank's system recognizes your IP address. The problem is that hackers can spoof your IP address and make your bank think that the hacker's computer is really yours. Enabling this feature you will save you from answering additional security questions every time you log on, but it is much riskier. Keep your security measures strong so you won't be the next hacking victim.

Here are some additional tips as provided by Naked Security, an award-winning newsroom with news, opinion, advice and research on computer security issues and the latest Internet threats:[186]

1. Choose an account with two-factor authentication, which is a process involving two stages to verify the identity of an entity trying to access services in a computer or in a network. Try to get a bank account that offers some form of two-factor authentication for online banking. These days many, but not all, banks offer a small device that can be used to generate a unique code each time you log in. This code is only valid for a very short period of time and is required in addition to your login credentials to gain access to your online account.

---

[186] Munson, Lee, "8 tips for safer online banking", *Naked Security*, Oct. 3, 2013 http://nakedsecurity.sophos.com/2013/10/03/8-tips-for-safer-online-banking/

2. When setting up online banking, if your bank asks you to provide answers to some standard security questions, remember that the answer you give doesn't have to be the real one. So you don't have to answer "Thumper" to the name of your first pet—make it something else, as if it was a password. Use a password manager if you are concerned about how to remember everything!

3. Secure your computer and keep it up-to-date. Security software is essential these days, regardless of how you use your computer. At a minimum, make sure you have a firewall turned on and are running antivirus software. You'll also want to keep your operating system and other software up to date to ensure that there are no security holes present.

4. Be wary of unsolicited phone calls that purport to be from your bank. While your financial institution may require you to answer a security question, they should never ask for passwords or PINs. They may ask for certain letters or numbers from them, but never the whole thing. If in doubt, do not be afraid to hang up and then call your bank back via a telephone number that you have independently confirmed as being valid.

5. It is always best practice to connect to your bank using computers and networks you know and trust. But if you need to access your bank online from remote locations, you might want to set up a VPN (Virtual Private Network) so that you can establish

an encrypted connection to your home or work network and access your bank from there. Look for a small padlock icon somewhere on your browser and check the address bar; the URL of the site you are on should begin with "https." Both act as confirmation that you are accessing your account over an encrypted connection.

6. It is also good practice to always log out of your online banking session when you have finished your business. This will lessen the chances of falling prey to session hijacking and cross-site scripting exploits. You may also want to take the extra precaution of setting up private browsing on your computer or Smartphone and set your browser to clear its cache at the end of each session.

7. Set up account notifications, if available. Some banks offer a facility for customers to set up text or email notifications to alert them to certain activities on their account. For example, if a withdrawal matches or exceeds a specified amount or the account balance dips below a certain point, then a message will be sent. Such alerts could give quick notice of suspicious activity in your account.

8. Monitor your accounts regularly. It should go without saying that monitoring your bank statement each month is good practice, but why wait a whole month to discover a discrepancy? With online banking, you have access 24/7, so take advantage of that and check your account on a regular basis. Look

at every transaction since you last logged in and, if you spot any anomalies, contact your bank immediately.

9. If you are used to going to your bank via a regular address and the address of the site you land at is not the same name, you can be confident that you are not at the real site. Always double check to make sure that the site address is accurate.

CHECK SCAMS

Fake check scams are clever ploys designed to steal your money. You can avoid becoming a victim by recognizing how the scam works and understanding your responsibility for the checks that you deposit in your account.

Beware if someone you don't know wants to pay you by check but wants you to wire some of the money back. It's a scam that could cost you thousands of dollars.

There has been an alarming increase in check scams, with new variations cropping up to trick even discerning consumers. It could start with someone offering to buy something you advertised, such as a car, boat or even pedigree dogs. They may offer to pay you to do work at home or negotiate with you on an apartment rental. Or you may have received a check claiming it's part of lottery money that has been deposited in a bank in your name. The possible scenarios are endless.

The key ingredient is that someone offers to send you a check, cashier's check or money order that is in excess of the amount you require. There is always an overpayment. Then they ask you to wire transfer some or all of the money out of your account or use a money transfer service such as Western Union®.

> Check fraud was the last thing on William Barker's mind when he reviewed his bank account balance to make sure his monthly retirement check had been deposited. It had arrived safely, but he noticed something else: A check for $4,500 had been cashed. It bore his wife's signature and a note that read "1984 motor home." There was just one problem: William and his wife didn't buy a 1984 motor home. When the doors of his bank opened that morning, Barker was there to dispute the transaction and begin the tedious process of recovering his money. Barker's bank ultimately restored the funds to his account, but he and his wife are still on guard for suspicious activity on all their accounts.[187]

WHAT CAN YOU DO?

Here are some things you can do to keep your checks safe from thieves and keep your personal information between you and your bank:

1. Review your checking accounts regularly for suspicious activity and reconcile your bank statement every month.

2. Keep your checks in a secure location. Don't leave them in a car, at work or out in the open at home.

---

[187] "Old-School Check Fraud Makes a Comeback", *Fox News*, Aug. 9, 2013, http://www.foxbusiness.com/personal-finance/2013/08/09/old-school-check-fraud-makes-comeback/

3. Drop bills paid with checks at the post office instead of in your mailbox.

4. Avoid having new checks sent by mail; pick them up at the bank.

5. Do not include personal data on your check. That includes your social security number, driver's license number, phone number and address.

6. Do not write your PIN number on your debit or ATM card or anywhere in your wallet or checkbook for a thief to find.

7. Shred old checks and bank statements before you throw them away.

8. Do not provide your bank information over the telephone

If you find a check has been fraudulently written on your account, be sure you do all four of these steps:

1. File a police report. You may need this for insurance purposes or to prove there was a theft.

2. Speak to the bank to dispute the check and close your account. You can open a new account and close your original account, which will prevent any additional transactions.

3. Place a 90-day alert on all three credit agencies, Equifax, TransUnion and Experian.

4. Go to the consumer assistance website ChexSystems to see if anyone has tried to open a new bank account with your personal information.[188]

If you have a complaint or problem involving a check written on, or deposited in an account at a national bank, and you cannot resolve the problem with the bank itself, contact the Office of the Comptroller of the Currency's Customer Assistance Group by calling (800) 613-6743 or by sending an e-mail to: customer.assistance@occ.treas.gov.

For mail-based scams, contact the U.S. Postal Inspector Service: by telephone at 1-888-877-7644; by mail at U.S. Postal Inspection Service, Office of Inspector General, Operations Support Group, 222 S. Riverside Plaza, Suite 1250, Chicago, IL 60606-6100; or via e-mail at https://postalinspectors.uspis.gov/forms/MailFraudComplai nt.aspx.

---

[188] https://www.consumerdebit.com/consumerinfo/us/en/index.htm

Chapter 11
NSA: The People Who Know Everything

If the National Security Agency (NSA) needs a slogan, it should probably be 'collect it all.' But the fight over whether that's an appropriate strategy for keeping order in a democratic society is one that stretches far beyond the NSA programs now being debated. We now have technologies that enable the creation of very detailed data on our activities. These technologies are only going to get more powerful and pervasive. We need to make a choice as a society about the extent to which we want to allow the government to store up that data so that it has the power to hit 'rewind' on everybody's lives. [189]

NATIONAL SECURITY AGENCY (NSA)

There are clearly three groups of people who are giving thought to the NSA and its mass data collection. First, there are those who really don't care because they rationalize they haven't done anything wrong; if the government has data about them, it's not a big deal. Second, there are those who think we must allow the government to have powerful surveillance techniques to protect against criminals and terrorists. And third, there are the people who are sure the

---

[189] Stanley, Jay, "From the NSA to License Plate Readers: Are We to Have a 'Collect It All' Society?" *ACLU Privacy and Technology Project*, June 26, 2013 https://www.aclu.org/blog/national-security-technology-and-liberty-free-speech/nsa-license-plate-readers-are-we-have

Orwellian prophesy of *1984* is here and who are fighting to turn back the government's spying powers.

The following graph shows the public's attitude on NSA spying in just two areas. Surprisingly the majority thought that the NSA was justified in monitoring phones but were a little more mistrustful of E-mail monitoring.

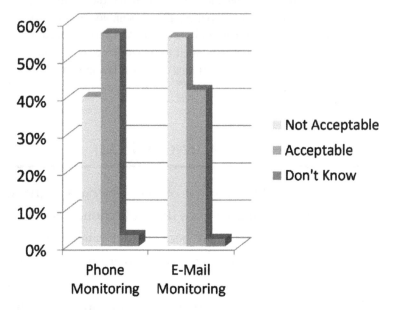

Public Attitudes toward NSA Spying—Pew Research[190]

Maybe the first group would care a little more if they realized the extent of the spying. Not only do the NSA and other government agencies collect phone and email records, they also collect financial transactions, hotel records, Google searches, images taken by street cameras, plane reservations, medical records, credit and debit card transactions—the list

[190] Pew Research, Jun 10, 2013, http://www.people-press.org/2013/06/10/majority-views-nsa-phone-tracking-as-acceptable-anti-terror-tactic/

goes on and on. While most of the people in this group are focused on illegal hackers, they forget that their government is also collecting sensitive information about them, their families, their friends and the people they do business with.

> ...[M]ore revelations pointed to NSA efforts to decrypt or surveil data as it traveled between the data centers of companies like Yahoo! and Google. Yet another program siphoned users' entire contact lists from services like Gmail, Yahoo! Mail, Hotmail and Facebook–NSA documents cited a single day when 82,857 contact lists were taken from Facebook users.[191]

> Documents seen and published by the New York Times show that the NSA can harvest information such as a person's age, location and sexual orientation from the data sent over the Internet by apps. Such personal details are contained in the data that apps send back to the companies that maintain and support them. This includes data sent to companies that serve and target ads in mobile apps. Google Maps was singled out as leaking particularly useful data for surveillance purposes. Documents from the NSA note how search queries intercepted from this app can reveal a person's movements.[192]

But let's move to the second group, who argue that we need to encourage the NSA in its data collection methods. One of those is Fareed Zakaria, noted author and host of *GPS* on

---

[191] Greenberg, Andy, "Zuckerberg Says He Called Obama To Express 'Frustration' Over NSA Surveillance". *Forbes*, March 13, 2014, http://www.forbes.com/sites/andygreenberg/2014/03/13/zuckerberg-says-he-called-obama-to-express-frustration-over-nsa-surveillance/

[192] Simonite, Tom, "U.S and U.K. surveillance of Smartphone users helped by mobile developers—few of whom bother to adopt basic encryption," *MIT Technology Review*, Jan 28, 2014, http://www.technologyreview.com/news/523971/how-app-developers-leave-the-door-open-to-nsa-surveillance/

CNN. He writes in *Time Magazine* that "The U.S.—its government, businesses and people—is under massive, sustained surveillance and infiltration by criminals, terrorists and foreign governments."[193] He points out that the theft of intellectual property and trade secrets from the U.S. networks is very prevalent, and utility companies have seen a tremendous rise in cyber-attacks. He states, "We all live, bank, work and play in a new parallel world of computer identities, data and transactions. But we do not seem to realize that this enormous freedom of activity in the cyberworld, as in the real world, has to be defended."[194]

Michelle Van Cleave, head of U.S. counterintelligence under President George W. Bush, asks, "Is our privacy being violated when computers churn through billions of strings of digital data looking for signals of terrorist activity? Or is that something that we need the government to do to keep us safe? Don't intrude but keep me safe. How to square such a circle? Today, when a personal video can 'go viral' in an instant, five hundred million people have a follow-me-right-this-second Twitter account, and some two billion people have access to the Internet, the digital records of U.S. citizens are comingled with the rest of the world in a maze of activity that is a fount of intelligence information."[195]

---

[193] Zakaria, Fareed, "The Case for Snooping", *Time*, February 3, 2014, pg. 22

[194] Zakaria, Fareed, ibid

[195] Van, Cleave, Michelle, "What It Takes: In Defense of the NSA", *World Affairs*, Dec. 2013, http://www.worldaffairsjournal.org/article/what-it-takes-defense-nsa

And she voices my own opinion about the flurry over the NSA in asking about the thousands of data brokers who are collecting even more data than our government. Of that, Van Cleave says, "I find the loss of privacy in today's digital world very troubling—but not because of the U.S. government. It's the cookies that enable some Web merchant to track what I buy online and send me tailored ads to buy more. It's the manner in which the Apple cloud insists on scooping up my entire personal calendar and contact information—and I can't opt out if I want my cell phone to work. It's the ever-vigilant, ever-ready Chinese microchip in my laptop computer, including the little extra that takes over the video camera and watches the room. Where is the public outrage about all of that?"[196]

Not a day goes by without several new articles about the NSA appearing in newspapers, magazines and blogs. Edward Snowden opened the door to heavy scrutiny of our intelligence gathering agencies—whether he should be considered a patriot or a traitor is still to be determined. Unfortunately, without massive surveillance, the government has no way of separating the "good" people from the "bad." If they could not track certain phrases or anomalies in conversations and online communications, potential attacks against critical transportation, power, water, communication, financial and other infrastructures would be almost impossible to detect.

The final group of people are those who are actively fighting to turn back the government's ability to collect and analyze

---

[196] Van Cleave, Michelle, ibid

any and all types of data about both its citizens and people in other countries. In the wake of the NSA revelations, there has been an avalanche of state bills requiring law enforcement to obtain a probable cause warrant before tracking an individual's location in an investigation. Most state legislators know they can't control the NSA—but they can control their state and local law enforcement agencies, which are engaging in some of the same invasive practices. The trend actually started in the wake of the ACLU's nationwide public records requests on location tracking and the 2013 U.S. v. Jones decision.[197]

The U.S. v. Jones was a landmark case in which the government had placed a GPS device on a defendant's car and tracked his movements for a month without a search warrant. It then justified its actions by arguing that the Fourth Amendment did not apply because the car was traveling on public streets. The court of appeals rejected that argument, stressing the intrusiveness of GPS technology and noting that tracking someone's movements over an extended period reveals a great deal about a person beyond his/her mere location at any particular moment.[198]

Supreme Court Justice Sonia Sotomayor makes this point in her concurring opinion in U.S. v. Jones. Citing the Smith ruling, she wrote:

---

[197] Bohm, Allie, "Status of Location Privacy Legislation in the U.S.", *ACLU, Apr 8, 2014, https://www.aclu.org/blog/technology-and-liberty-national-security/status-location-privacy-legislation-states*

[198] U.S. v. Jones Decided, American Civil Liberties Union, Jul 18, 2012, https://www.aclu.org/technology-and-liberty/us-v-jones

"It may be necessary to reconsider the premise that an individual has no reasonable expectation of privacy in information voluntarily disclosed to third parties. This approach is ill suited to the Digital Age, in which people reveal a great deal of information about themselves to third parties in the course of carrying out mundane tasks. People disclose the phone numbers that they dial or text to their cellular providers; the URLs that they visit and the e-mail addresses with which they correspond to their Internet service providers; and the books, groceries, and medications they purchase to online retailers. Perhaps, as Justice Alito notes, some people may find the 'tradeoff' of privacy for convenience 'worthwhile,' or come to accept this 'diminution of privacy' as 'inevitable,' and perhaps not. I for one doubt that people would accept without complaint the warrantless disclosure to the Government of a list of every Web site they had visited in the last week, or month, or year."[199]

Justice Sotomayor also worries that citizens might choose not to attend certain political, cultural or religious events for fear of being publicly associated with a group or idea.

EXPLOITING VULNERABILITIES

Heartbleed is a very far-reaching cyber-security scare, and experts say data will continue to be difficult to secure. By one estimate, as much as 66% of the Web is affected,

---

[199] Serwer, Adam, "How Sotomayer undermined Obama's NSA", *MSNBC*, Dec 23, 2013, http://www.msnbc.com/msnbc/how-sotomayor-undermined-obamas-nsa

including Yahoo! and OKCupid. "There are no secrets on the Internet," says Ari Takanen, who works for the security firm that discovered Heartbleed. "Something bad can always happen."[200]

> The U.S. National Security Agency knew for at least two years about a flaw in the way that many websites send sensitive information, now dubbed the Heartbleed bug, and regularly used it to gather critical intelligence, people familiar with the matter said. The agency's reported decision to keep the bug secret in pursuit of national security interests threatens to renew the rancorous debate over the role of the government's top computer experts. The NSA, after declining to comment on the report, subsequently denied that it was aware of Heartbleed until the vulnerability was made public by a private security report earlier this month.[201]

The Heartbleed bug allows anyone on the Internet to read the memory of the systems protected by the vulnerable versions of the Open SSL software. This compromises the secret keys used to identify the service providers and to encrypt the traffic, the names and passwords of the users and the actual content. It allows attackers to eavesdrop on communications, steal data directly from the services and users and to impersonate services and users.[202]

Critics accuse the NSA of exploiting Heartbleed to obtain passwords and other basic data that are the building blocks of the sophisticated hacking operations at the core of its

[200] Luckerson, Victor, "Time to Change Your Password. Again." *Time*, Apr 11, 2014, Pg. 14

[201] Riley, Michael, "NSA Said to Exploit Heartbleed Bug for Intelligence for Years", *Bloomberg*, Apr 11, 2014, http://www.bloomberg.com/news/2014-04-11/nsa-said-to-have-used-heartbleed-bug-exposing-consumers.html

[202] Information posted on *Heartbleed*, http://heartbleed.com/

mission at a cost to millions of ordinary users who were left vulnerable to attack from criminal hackers. The NSA devotes millions of dollars and has over 1,000 experts devoted to hunting for common software flaws that are critical to stealing data from secure computers. Open-source protocols like OpenSSL, where the flaw was found, are primary targets. The agency found Heartbleed shortly after its introduction, according to one of the people familiar with the matter.[203]

The public may be placing too much trust in software and hardware developers to insure the security of our most sensitive transactions. Currently, the NSA has a trove of thousands of such vulnerabilities that can be used to breach some of the world's most sensitive computers, according to a person briefed on the matter.[204]

> Since 2010, the NSA has used data it gathered to map some Americans' social connections to identify their associates, their locations, their travel companions and other personal information. The NSA was authorized to conduct "large-scale graph analysis on very large sets of communications metadata without having to check foreignness," according to an NSA memorandum reported in the New York Times. The agency reportedly used material from GPS coordinates, along with Facebook and other social media profiles in their analysis.[205]

---

[203] Riley, Michael, Ibid

[204] Riley, Michael, Ibid

[205] Risen James & Poitras, Laura, "NSA Gathers Data on Social Connections of U.S. Citizens", *New York Times*, Sep 28, 2013 http://www.nytimes.com/2013/09/29/us/nsa-examines-social-networks-of-us-citizens.html?pagewanted=all&_r=0

THE "NEW" NSA

President Barack Obama, who initially defended the National Security Agency's surveillance and data collection programs, branding them a "modest encroachment" on privacy for the good of national defense, has since endorsed a plan to change the NSA's data collection.

The general idea is to end the government storage of phone metadata by transferring that storage to private phone companies. Under the administration's proposal, the government must obtain a judge's approval before accessing phone records, though exceptions could be made in cases of national security emergencies. The NSA's database includes phone numbers that are called and the duration of those calls, but does not include the content of phone calls. NSA analysts will have to get a court order to obtain information from phone company databases except in cases where NSA officials can authorize searches on their own so long as they have a "reasonably articulated suspicion" that a particular number is involved in terrorist activities.[206]

The NSA will still have broad authority to intercept email and other Internet communications overseas, which often involve Americans who communicate with foreigners or are traveling overseas. When Americans' communications are intercepted, the NSA is allowed to keep that information if it is relevant to a terrorism investigation or other foreign

---

[206] Lauter, David, "NSA surveillance: What's changing, what isn't", *LA Times*, Jan 17, 2014, http://www.latimes.com/nation/politics/politicsnow/la-pn-obama-nsa-speech-reforms-breakdown-20140117,0,4190308.story#ixzz2yWYjSdK6

intelligence purpose, but is required to "minimize" how that information gets shared with other government agencies. [207]

NSA opponents say that the new proposal is only designed to placate the American people and really doesn't stop the NSA from collecting what they want. Just because phone records will now be stored "off site" doesn't mean the NSA won't have ready access to them when they feel a need to sift through conversations.

Reacting to reports that the NSA knew about encryption vulnerabilities like Heartbleed, President Barack Obama convened a panel to review surveillance activities and suggest reforms. Among the dozens of changes put forward was a recommendation that the NSA quickly move to fix software flaws rather than exploit them and that they be used only in "rare instances" and for short periods of time.[208]

WHAT CAN YOU DO?

To educate the public, the ACLU has launched a NSA Document website that lists all the documents made public since June 2013. They state, "We have made all of the documents text-searchable to allow users to investigate particular key words or phrases. Alternatively, the filter function allows users to sort based on the type of surveillance involved, the specific legal authorities

---

[207] Lauter, David, Ibid

[208] Riley, Michael, Ibid

implicated, the purpose of the surveillance, or the source of the disclosure. The fact is that most of the documents contained in this database should have never been secret in the first place. Now, with newfound access to these records, we can educate ourselves about the true nature and scope of government surveillance in its many forms. This database will serve as a critical tool with which we will hold our government accountable."[209]

Responding to news reports that the National Security Agency may be monitoring more online activity than was previously believed, Microsoft launched what they are calling a comprehensive engineering effort to enhance encryption on communications via tools like its e-mail service Outlook, productivity suite Office 365, SkyDrive and Windows Azure. The company said it is rolling out three new features: 1) Expanded encryption across Microsoft services, 2) Reinforced legal protections for customer data and 3) Enhanced transparency designed to show customers that Microsoft products don't have "back doors" that make government surveillance easier.[210]

Other software companies like Google and Yahoo! are also tightening up their encryption of users' data. Mark Zuckenberg, CEO of Facebook, alleged that the National

[209] Weinrebe, Emily, "Introducing the ACLU's NSA Documents Database", ACLU National Security Project, Apr 3, 2014, https://www.aclu.org/blog/national-security/introducing-aclus_nsa-documents-database

[210] Gross, Doug, "Microsoft fights back against NSA snooping", *CNN*, Dec 9, 2013, http://www.cnn.com/2013/12/05/tech/web/microsoft-nsa-snooping/

Security Agency went "way over the line" by hiding its surveillance programs from the American people.[211]

The debate goes on. The group of people who think the NSA are the "thought police" claim the government's efforts to intensify its surveillance through backdoors, weak encryption and other intelligence-gathering tools are threats to Internet security. The group that defends the NSA, including the U.S. Intelligence chiefs, has said the country's ability to spot terrorist threats and understand the intent of hostile leaders would be vastly diminished if the practice of monitoring emails and the exploitation of vulnerabilities were prohibited. And the group that doesn't care because they feel they won't be monitored still remains in the majority.

No matter which side ultimately prevails, it remains a fact that the NSA has contradictory roles: the defensive role to protect U.S. computer networks from any attack, and the offensive role of searching for and utilizing vulnerabilities to monitor terrorist and hacker activities throughout the world. As stated previously, the NSA remains firm in their belief that in order to protect America, its citizens must be willing to give up a certain amount of personal privacy.

---

[211] Briefing, *Time*, March 10, 2014 pg. 8

Conclusion

The goal of this book was to increase your awareness of the many ways each of us give away personal information every day, usually without even realizing it. In many instances, we cannot control how this information is used by others. After reading this book, however, you have learned that there are many opportunities to protect your privacy and take control of some of your personal information.

Some of the suggestions we provided seem like common sense, but others take a little more effort on your part. Here are the main items you should consider:

1. Use strong passwords.

2. Limit the information you post on social media sites.

3. Be aware that your driving habits are being observed through license plate scans and your car's telematics.

4. Never subscribe to unsolicited credit cards.

5. Monitor your credit on all three nationwide credit bureaus.

6. Limit your use of debit cards.

7. Understand how your personal information is revealed to marketing and data brokers and opt out

of data sharing whenever you are given the opportunity.

8. Sign up for the Do Not Call list.

9. Protect your personal information on your Smartphone by using the security lockout feature.

10. Shred documents containing financial or personally identifiable information such as your social security number to prevent identity theft.

11. Only donate to charities you know give the majority of the donation to the needy—not to marketing companies.

12. Understand your right to access your medical records and keep a close check on suspicious statements.

13. Make a list of your digital assets and determine if you need to include them in your will.

14. Read the privacy policies from your bank and investment firm and opt out of any customer data sharing.

15. Never open an email from an unknown source.

You may have to adopt some new habits, but the more you protect your data the better you will sleep at night, knowing you have done all you can to insure your privacy. We can't guarantee you won't ever be hacked, but monitoring your accounts will allow you to shut down any breaches quickly with a minimum of damage and aggravation.

Glossary

Algorithm is a finite set of step-by-step instructions for a problem-solving or computation procedure. For security transactions, it is one that can be implemented by a computer.

Cache is when you visit a webpage and the browser caches (stores) the HTML, images or files referenced by the page. When you browse through other pages on that site, your browser will not have to re-download the files. Instead, the browser can simply load them from the cache, which is stored on your local hard drive.

Chex Systems, Inc. is a network comprised of member financial Institutions that regularly contribute information on mishandled checking and savings accounts to a central location. ChexSystems shares this information among member institutions to help them assess the risk of opening new accounts. There are certain reports a consumer can request free of charge if they think their checking account has been compromised.

Computer Virus is a program that, when executed, replicates by inserting copies of itself into other computer programs, data files or the hard drive of your computer. When this replication succeeds, the affected areas are then said to be "infected." Viruses often perform some type of harmful activity on infected hosts, such as stealing hard disk space or CPU time, accessing private information, corrupting data or sometimes bringing down whole computer systems.

Cookie is a small piece of data sent from a website and stored in a user's Web browser while the user is browsing that website. Every time the user loads the website, the browser sends the cookie back to the server to notify the website of the user's previous activity.

Cybercrime is criminal activity or a crime committed by means of computers or the Internet. The most prominent form of cybercrime is identity theft.

Data Breach is an incident in which sensitive, protected or confidential data has potentially been viewed, stolen or used by an individual unauthorized to do so. Data breaches may involve personal health information (PHI), personally identifiable information (PII), trade secrets or intellectual property.

Data Integrity refers to the state that exists when computerized data is the same as the data in the original or source document and has not been exposed to malicious or accidental alteration.

Digital Asset refers to any item of text or media that has been formatted into a binary source and includes the right to use it. A digital file without the right to use it is not an asset.

Exploit is a virus that exploits weaknesses in computer systems to gain unauthorized access to applications and files. An exploit takes advantage of a bug, glitch or vulnerability in order to cause unintended or unanticipated behavior to occur on computer software or hardware and frequently gains control of a computer system. You may have an exploit on your computer system if you see strange and sudden pop-ups, programs crashing or your system rebooting without prompting.

Fair Credit Reporting Act (FCRA) is the main law for consumers and companies as it relates to the U.S. credit reporting system. It not only protects consumers by specifying their rights, but it also lists the responsibilities of companies who collect the credit information, distribute the credit reports and use the information.

Federal Deposit Insurance Corporation (FDIC) is the U.S. Corporation insuring deposits in the U.S. against bank failure. The FDIC was created in 1933 to maintain public confidence and encourage stability in the financial system through the promotion of sound banking practices.

Firewall is a software or hardware-based network security system that controls incoming and outgoing network traffic based on a set of rules. A firewall establishes a barrier between a trusted, secure internal network and another network (e.g., the Internet) that may not be secure and trusted.

Foreign Intelligence Surveillance Court (FISA Court) authorizes government requests for wiretapping, data analysis and other electronic surveillance of suspected terrorists and spies operating in the United States for "foreign intelligence purposes." To collect the information, the government has to demonstrate to a judge that it is "relevant" to an international terrorism investigation.

Hashing is a technique for locating data in a file by applying a transformation, usually arithmetic, to a key. A **hash function** is any algorithm that maps data of variable length to data of a fixed length. The values returned by a hash function are called **hash values** and are used in many encryption algorithms.

HTML stands for "Hyper-Text Markup Language." This is the language that Web pages are written in. Also known as hypertext documents, Web pages must conform to the rules of HTML in order to be displayed correctly in a Web browser.

Internet Protocol (IP) address is a unique identifier for each computer or other device on a network including the Internet. IP addresses are a string of numbers that allow computers, routers, printers and other devices to recognize or identify one another and communicate.

Keylogging is the practice of using a software program or hardware device (keylogger) to record all keystrokes on a computer keyboard, either overtly as a surveillance tool or covertly as spyware. Some employers make use of keylogging to monitor their employees' computer habits.

Malware is an abbreviation for malicious software, or software used to disrupt computer operations, gather sensitive information or gain hostile access to computer systems. Malware is a general term used to refer to a variety of types of intrusive software.

Metadata is data that describes other data. It summarizes basic information about data, which can make finding and working with particular instances of data easier. For example, author, date created and file size are examples of very basic document metadata and makes it much easier for someone to locate a specific document.

Network, or computer network, is a group of two or more computers connected by cables or wireless signals that can communicate with one another. Networks can also include other devices such as printers, routers and network hubs.

Pharming is a way hackers redirect users to false websites without them even knowing it by means of a virus that changes or modifies the user's host files.

Phishing is used by scammers and is the practice of sending out e-mails that appear to come from legitimate websites such as banking institutions. The e-mails state that your information needs to be updated or validated and ask that you enter your username and password by clicking a false link included in the e-mail.

Salt is a random string of data that is used as additional input to a one-way function that hashes a password or pass-phrase. A new salt is randomly generated for each password. Typically, the salt and the password are concatenated and processed with a hash function that takes an arbitrary block of data and returns a fixed size bit string called a cryptographic hash value. The resulting output (but not the original password) is stored with the salt in a database. Hashing allows for later authentication while defending against any compromises of the password in the event that the database is hacked or compromised by an unknown source.

Social Engineering is a method of deceiving users into divulging private information by taking advantage of our natural tendency to trust one another rather than relying solely on technological means to steal information. It is often associated with phishing, pharming, spam and other Internet-based scams.

Spam is unsolicited electronic mail advertising. Most state anti-spam laws prohibit misrepresenting or falsifying the origin of or the routing information on messages, using an Internet address of a third party without permission or including misleading information in the subject line of a message.

Spyware is a type of software that gathers information about a person or organization without their knowledge. This information may then be sent to another location without the owner's consent. Spyware can also control a computer without the owner's knowledge. Five types of spyware include monitors, cameras, trojans, adware and tracking cookies. Advertisers use a type of spyware to track and store Internet users' movements on the Web, serving up pop-up ads to potential buyers. Recently, the term "Spyware" has been used to describe the NSA's gathering of personal information through Internet sites.

Stingray is an electronic surveillance device for remotely capturing data from mobile telephones. It is designed to simulate a cell tower and capture information, including location data, which can be done even when the phone is not being used to make a call. A stingray can be carried by hand or mounted on a vehicle such as an unmanned aerial vehicle.

Stored Communications Act (SCA) is a law that addresses voluntary and compelled disclosure of "stored wire and electronic communications and transactional records" held by third-party Internet service providers (ISPs). ISPs are forbidden to divulge the contents of any communication which is carried or maintained on that service.

Trojan is a non-self-replicating type of malware that gains privileged access to the operating system, usually as a backdoor, allowing unauthorized access to the target's computer. Trojans are not computer viruses but are there to steal information. Trojans can be installed via online games or Internet-driven applications, and you probably won't know they are there except that your computer may slow down.

Vehicle Telematics includes, but is not limited to, Global Positioning System (GPS) technology integrated with computers and mobile communications technology in automotive navigation systems. Telematics is often used for vehicle tracking of the location, movement, status and behavior of a vehicle or fleet of vehicles.

 Web pages make up the World Wide Web. These documents are written in HTML and are translated by your Web browser. A **website** is a collection of Web pages.

Sources for Additional Info

AMERICAN CIVIL LIBERTIES UNION (ACLU)

Articles on Car Tracking, Surveillance & Privacy, Internet & Consumer Privacy: https://www.aclu.org/key-issues

BUREAU OF CONSUMER PROTECTION

Free resource on consumer privacy, credit reporting, data security, Children's Online Privacy Protection Act (COPPA), the Gramm-Leach-Bliley Act for financial institutions and more: http://www.business.ftc.gov/privacy-and-security

EUROPEAN COMMISSION ON JUSTICE

Common EU rules that have been established to ensure personal data has high standards of protection within the EU, and specific rules for the transfer of personal data outside the EU: http://ec.europa.eu/justice/data-protection/index_en.htm

FEDERAL TRADE COMMISSION (FTC) IDENTITY THEFT OR INFORMATION ABOUT THE FAIR CREDIT REPORTING ACT (FCRA)

A national resource to help you deter, detect and defend against identity theft. And to learn more about FCRA:

http://www.consumer.ftc.gov/features/feature-0014-identity-theft or

http://www.consumer.ftc.gov/topics/credit-and-loans

HEALTH & HUMAN SERVICES DEPARTMENT

If you believe that a medical provider or someone who works for a medical provider violated your (or someone else's) health information privacy rights, you may file a complaint with Office of Civil Rights (OCR). Get more info by emailing OCRComplaint@hhs.gov

IDENTITY THEFT ASSISTANCE CENTER (ITAC)

A nonprofit, collaborative effort between financial institutions and law enforcement to provide you with tools and information for preventing and detecting fraud and identity theft: http://www.identitytheftassistance.org/

IDENTITY THEFT RESOURCE CENTER (ITRC)

Step-by-step resolution instructions, form letters and other resources to assist identity theft victims: http://www.idtheftcenter.org/

INFORMATION COMMISSIONERS OFFICE (ICO)

An independent authority set up to uphold information rights in the UK by promoting openness by public bodies and data privacy for individuals: http://ico.org.uk/for_organisations/data_protection/the_guide

ISO/IEC 27000:2009 (E). INFORMATION TECHNOLOGY - SECURITY TECHNIQUES - INFORMATION SECURITY MANAGEMENT SYSTEMS - OVERVIEW AND VOCABULARY

Provides an overview of information security management systems that are the subject of the information security management system (ISMS) family of standards, and defines related terms: http://www.iso27001security.com/html/27000.html

NATIONAL CONFERENCE OF STATE LEGISLATORS

State Laws related to Internet privacy. This site lists laws by state, and additional resources for privacy legislation: http://www.ncsl.org/research/telecommunications-and-information-technology/state-laws-related-to-internet-privacy

NATIONAL SECURITY ARCHIVE OF GEORGE WASHINGTON UNIVERSITY

Documents, news, publications and research. The Archive collects and publishes declassified documents acquired through the Freedom of Information Act (FOIA): http://www2.gwu.edu/~nsarchiv/index.html

NATIONAL INSTITUTE OF STANARDS & TECHNOLOGY (NIST) COMPUTER SECURITY DIVISION

Shares information about security tools and practices. Information about security standards and guidelines and key security web resources: http://csrc.nist.gov/

PRIVACY INTERNATIONAL

Their stated objectives are "Promoting the right to privacy and data protection in the development and humanitarian fields," and "Exposing the global trade in surveillance technologies and holding it to account": http://www.privacyinternational.org

U.S. SMALL BUSINESS ADMINISTRATION

Information on how your business can comply with privacy laws and children's online privacy: http://www.sba.gov/content/privacy-law

U.S. DEPARTMENT OF JUSTICE

Global Privacy Resources site is a roadmap that guides justice entities through the diverse privacy policy development and implementation products available today: http://it.ojp.gov/privacy

U.S. DEPARTMENT OF THE TREASURY

Office of the Comptroller of the Currency for information about the Federal Banking System including Fraud Resources: http://www.occ/gov/index.html

WIKIPEDIA

Definitions and other helpful information about personal and data security: http://en.wikipedia.org/wiki/Information_security